1 - Focus on Catholicism

FOCUS ON CATHOLICISM

FOCUS ON CATHOLICISM

Catholic Belief And Practice

*

EDWARD J. GRATSCH

ALBA · HOUSE NEW · YORK

SOCIETY OF ST. PAUL, 2187 VICTORY BLVD., STATEN ISLAND, NEW YORK 10314

Library of Congress Cataloging-in-Publication Data

Gratsch, Edward J.
Focus on Catholicism : Catholic belief and practice /
Edward J. Gratsch.
p. cm.
Includes bibliographical references.
ISBN 0-8189-0562-X
1. Catholic Church — Doctrines. I. Title.
BX1754.G696 1989 89-36829
282 — dc20 CIP

Nihil Obstat:
Christopher R. Armstrong
November 7, 1988

Imprimatur:
Most Rev. James H. Garland
Auxiliary Bishop of Cincinnati
November 11, 1988

Designed, printed and bound in the United States of America by the Fathers and Brothers of the Society of St. Paul, 2187 Victory Boulevard, Staten Island, New York 10314, as part of their communications apostolate.

Printing Information:

Current Printing - first digit 1 2 3 4 5 6 7 8 9 10 11 12

Year of Current Printing - first year shown
1989 1990 1991 1992 1993 1994 1995 1996

ACKNOWLEDGMENTS

Quotations from the Second Vatican Council are taken from *The Documents of Vatican II*, Abbot-Gallagher edition. Reprinted with the permission of America Press Inc., 106 West 56th Street, New York, NY 10019. All rights reserved.

All Scripture texts are taken from *The New American Bible*, copyright 1970 by the Confraternity of Christian Doctrine, Washington, DC, including the Revised New Testament, copyright 1986, and are used by permission of the copyright owner. All rights reserved.

CONTENTS

Part I
CATHOLIC BELIEF

Part II
CATHOLIC PRACTICE

INTRODUCTION

This book originated as a series of talks delivered over radio station WCKY in Cincinnati, Ohio. The series of talks was called *Focus On Catholicism.* In these talks I intended to explain Catholic belief and practice primarily for the benefit of Catholics so that they might understand better the faith they live by. However, I also intended to explain Catholic belief and practice for the benefit of non-Catholics who might wish to learn more about Catholicism. I received a good many favorable comments about the talks from my listening audience, so I decided to publish them in this form.

In this book I have preserved the material as talks to a radio audience. I believe they have, therefore, a personal quality which they might otherwise lack. Moreover, because these talks were composed to be read aloud by the speaker, there is a certain similarity, however remote, between them and the manuscripts of the New Testament, which were also meant to be read aloud. When they were composed, most people could not read, so someone had to read them aloud for the benefit of most Christians.

I have placed some questions for review at the end of each talk. These questions serve to focus attention on the principal points of the talk. The questions might also serve as a point of departure for a discussion in case a group might use this book for common study. Each talk reflects the fifteen minute time frame within which it was delivered. If my *Focus On Catholicism* contributes to a deeper understanding of "the faith delivered once for all to the saints" (Jude 3), I shall be amply rewarded.

EDWARD J. GRATSCH

PART I

CATHOLIC BELIEF

CHAPTER 1

GOD

It is my intention to speak to you in the weeks to come about Catholic belief and practice. To begin with, I plan to speak about Catholic belief; and then I shall take up Catholic practice, for what one believes should determine what one does. I shall start at the very beginning, that is to say, with God, and specifically, with the existence of God.

Can we prove that God exists? By God I mean the Supreme Being, the Being perfect in power, wisdom, and glory, whom human beings worship as Creator and Ruler of the universe.

In my judgment, the famous five ways drawn up by St. Thomas Aquinas in the thirteenth century demonstrate the existence of God from the things that he has made. These five ways proceed from a simple fact of experience; for example, the motion of a leaf in the wind, the birth of an animal, or the regular movement of the earth around the sun. By invoking the principle of causality, St. Thomas comes to the conclusion that there must be a first mover, a first cause, an absolutely necessary being, a supreme being, an architect and governor of the universe, whom we call God.

Further analysis leads St. Thomas to conclude that God is endowed with all those attributes that we associate with divinity — in other words, that God is utterly perfect, good, present everywhere, unchangeable, eternal, one, all-knowing, and all-powerful. In this way, St. Thomas arrives at the theistic conception of God. In my judgment and in the judgment of many others too, the reasoning of St. Thomas Aquinas is as rigorous as that of a mathematician or scientist.

Let me give you an example of Thomas' third way of proving the existence of God. Notice that the things that go to make up the world as we know it are not the products of themselves, but the products of something else. The rug on the floor, the tree in the park, the mineral in the soil, the bird in the nest, men and women — all these things are not the product of themselves, but of something else. Moreover, just as one thing in this world cannot explain its existence without reference to something else, so the entire universe, which is the sum total of its parts, cannot explain its existence without reference to something radically distinct from it. Therefore, to explain the world as we know it, we must suppose the existence of a Being, which is not the product of something else, a Being whom we call God.

Allow me to give you an example of Thomas' fifth way of proving the existence of God. It reasons from the order observed in the universe to a supreme intelligence from which that order is derived. Have you ever seen an orrery or a picture of one? An orrery is an apparatus that shows the relative positions and motions of bodies in the solar system. When the wheels turn and the arms move, one can see just how the planets move around the sun and their relation to each other. Common sense tells us that some intelligent being made the orrery. So, too, common sense tells us that some intelligent being directs the solar system of which the orrery is a model. This intelligent being we call God.

The Bible indicates that God can be known from his works. For example, we read in the Old Testament Book of Wisdom (13:5) that the greatness and beauty of created things reveal their original author. And Paul writes in his Letter to the Romans that "ever since the creation of the world, his [God's] invisible attributes of eternal power and divinity have been able to be understood and perceived in what he has made" (Rm 1:20). Thomas Aquinas' arguments for the existence of God show how God can be known from his works, as transcending his works.

I venture to say, though, that for most Christians, including Catholics, the teaching of Jesus about the existence of God is decisive. They reason, consciously or unconsciously, somewhat in this fashion: Jesus asserted the existence of God; but Jesus demonstrated superhuman goodness, wisdom, and power. He knew whereof he spoke and he did not try to deceive. Since Jesus affirmed the existence of God, God must exist.

I think too that Jesus is largely responsible for shaping the Christian's conception of God. What was Jesus' idea of God? What attributes or characteristics did he associate with divinity?

In his Sermon on the Mount, as it is recorded in Matthew's Gospel, Jesus described in some detail the attributes of God.

In that sermon, Jesus taught us to think of God as our Father: "This is how you are to pray, 'Our Father in heaven, hallowed be your name. . . .' " (Mt 6:9).

In the Sermon on the Mount, Jesus taught us that God takes care of us: "Look at the birds in the sky; they do not sow or reap, they gather nothing into barns, yet your heavenly Father feeds them. Are not you more important than they?" (Mt 6:26).

In the Sermon on the Mount, Jesus reminded us that God knows our secret thoughts and deeds. Jesus encouraged us to give alms without fanfare and to pray in the privacy of our room. And he concluded: "Your Father who sees in secret will repay you" (Mt 6:4-6).

In that same sermon, Jesus spoke of God as perfect: "So be perfect, just as your heavenly Father is perfect" (Mt 5:48).

Elsewhere in the gospels, Jesus described other attributes of God. For Jesus, God is worthy of total love. Speaking to the lawyer, Jesus approved the injunction of the Old Testament: "You shall love the Lord, your God, with all your heart, with all your being, with all your strength, and with all your mind, and your neighbor as yourself" (Lk 10:25-28; cf. Lv 19:18; Dt 6:5).

God is all-powerful. Speaking to his disciples about the danger of riches, Jesus said, "All things are possible for God" (Mt 10:27). Even a rich man can be saved.

According to Jesus, God is a forgiving God: "If you forgive others their transgressions, your heavenly Father will forgive you, but if you do not forgive others, neither will your Father forgive your transgressions" (Mt 6:14-15).

According to Jesus, God is a Spirit. Talking with the Samaritan woman at the well, Jesus said, "God is Spirit, and those who worship him must worship in Spirit and truth" (Jn 4:24).

For Jesus, God is alive: "Just as the Father has life in himself, so also he gave to his Son the possession of life in himself" (Jn 5:26).

I could go on at much greater length defining Jesus' conception of God; and I believe Jesus' idea of God has been most influential in the lives of Catholics. There is, however, a marvelous correspondence between Jesus' conception of God and the conclusions which St. Thomas reached purely on the basis of rational argumentation.

Still, there are atheists, men and women who deny the existence of God. The Second Vatican Council, a great gathering of Catholic bishops in the 1960's, considered atheism to be one of the most serious problems of this age. The bishops of the Council singled out two important reasons, among others, for modern atheism.

One reason is the desire for independence which some modern men and women experience. They wish to be the sole artisans and creators of their lives. Such a desire for independence cannot be reconciled with the affirmation of a Lord who is the Author and purpose of all things.

A second reason for modern atheism, according to the bishops of the Second Vatican Council, is the conviction in the minds of many that belief in God thwarts the social and economic emancipation of human beings. The Marxists hold this view. They hold that belief in God distracts the human race from the needs of the poor and oppressed of this world. [1]

What is to be said in response to these objections to the existence of God? A number of thoughts occur to me. If God exists, as he does, if he has made certain demands upon the human race, as I believe he has, then men and women simply cannot ignore God. Furthermore, even though men and women may feel independent and self-sufficient in certain situations, they necessarily feel helpless in the face of suffering which they cannot relieve, and in the face of death which they cannot overcome. In the face of unrelieved suffering and death, either modern men and women must bow down in defeat or else turn to God, who alone can render death and suffering meaningful. Finally, the recognition of God should not distract men and women from the needs of others, for we serve God by serving others.

1 Constitution on the Church in the Modern World, no. 20.

QUESTIONS FOR REVIEW

1. How does St. Thomas Aquinas argue for the existence of God?
2. What was Jesus' conception of God?
3. What are some reasons for modern atheism? What can be said in reply?

CHAPTER 2

THE HOLY TRINITY

Our thoughts today turn to a consideration of the Holy Trinity.

Since the revelation of God to the human race through Jesus of Nazareth, Christians have firmly believed that God is simultaneously *one* and *three* — one God in three divine persons. This is the mystery of the Holy Trinity. The three divine persons are the Father, Son, and Holy Spirit. The three divine persons are really distinct from one another. Each one is eternal and perfectly equal to the other two, yet they are one and the same God because all have one and the same divine nature. Of these three persons, the Son proceeds from the Father by an eternal generation; and the Holy Spirit proceeds from the Father and the Son by an eternal spiration, as it is called.

There is absolutely no way in which we could have come to the knowledge of the Holy Trinity by ourselves. We know about the three divine persons in the one God only because God has chosen to reveal them to us through Jesus. Even after the revelation of this mystery, we cannot understand it fully; but we believe it because we have God's word for it. The Christian teaching about the most Holy Trinity calls for acceptance, not understanding. This teaching reminds us that God is mystery. If we with our finite minds could comprehend God, he would not be infinite, as he is. We finite men and women are confronted by mystery when we reflect on ourselves. It is not surprising that we are confronted by mystery when we reflect on the infinite God. In heaven we shall see God face to face, and then we shall understand more fully how there are three divine persons in the one God.

God did not reveal the mystery of the Holy Trinity in a single blinding flash, but only gradually. There was a development between the Old and New Testaments. In the Old Testament God spoke to the nation of Israel and stressed his oneness. God commanded Moses to say: "Hear, O Israel! The Lord is our God, the Lord alone! Therefore, you shall love the Lord, your God, with all your heart, and with all your soul, and with all your strength" (Dt 6:4-5). In the New Testament, Jesus acknowledged that commandment as the first and greatest of the Lord's commandments (Mt 22:34-40). Jesus, the new Moses, preached an unyielding monotheism.

At the same time he taught us that God is one in three. We note the paradox of Jesus' teaching with respect to God the Father and himself. Jesus asserted his distinction from his heavenly Father. For example, speaking to his disciples, Jesus referred to God as "my Father" and "your Father" (Mt 7:21; 5:16). Jesus was the beloved Son of the Father (Mk 1:11). As the Son, Jesus has an incomparable intimacy with the Father: "No one knows the Son except the Father, and no one knows the Father except the Son. . . ." (Mt 11:27; Lk 10:22). Being the Son, therefore, Jesus is clearly distinct from God the Father.

Yet Jesus claimed divinity and equality with God the Father. Like God, Jesus forgave sins (Mk 2:1-12) and claimed to be Lord of the sabbath (Mk 2:28). Jesus modified the Law given by God in the Old Testament (Mt 5). In John's Gospel we hear the words of Jesus, "The Father and I are one" (Jn 10:30), and Jesus applies to himself the Hebrew name of God (Jn 8:58). Jesus asserted his distinction from God the Father, and yet he affirmed his identity with him.

The revelation of the Holy Spirit as a divine person is an

important theme of John's Gospel, of the Acts of the Apostles, and of the Epistles of Paul. In the fourteenth, fifteenth, and sixteenth chapters of John's Gospel, for example, we recognize that the Holy Spirit is not some thing, but Someone. We recognize that the Spirit is uniquely and intimately associated with both the Father and the Son; that he will be to the disciples what Jesus was to them; that he is, as Christ was, antagonistic to the world; that he will carry the salvific work of Christ to completion. Thus Jesus and the New Testament propound a mystery for our belief; three distinct persons are divine, but they are not three gods, only one God.

The mystery of the Holy Trinity has been expressed in the great creeds of the Church. For example, the Athanasian Creed of the fifth or sixth century puts the matter in this way: "The Father is God, the Son is God, and the Holy Spirit is God. But there are not three gods, only one God. The Father is Lord, the Son is Lord, and the Holy Spirit is Lord. But there are not three lords, only one Lord. For, according to Christian truth, we must profess that each of the persons individually is God; and according to the Christian religion we are forbidden to say that there are three gods or three lords. The Father is not made by anyone, nor generated by anyone. The Son is not made nor created, but he is generated by the Father alone. The Holy Spirit is not made, nor created, nor generated, but proceeds from the Father and the Son."[1]

Frequently we resort to examples to clarify the mystery of the Holy Trinity as far as we can. Just as the three angles of a triangle are distinct from one another, yet each angle embraces, as it were, the whole area of the triangle, so the three persons of the Holy Trinity are distinct from one another, yet each person is identified with the nature of God. Just as a child is the expression of the love between father and mother, so the Holy Spirit is the expression of the love between Father and

1 *The Christian Faith* (New York: Alba House, 1982), p. 12, no. 16.

0Son. A third and final example. Just as the mind, the hand, and the instrument of the musician produce the musical sound, so Father, Son, and Holy Spirit have created and sustain the harmony of the universe. Even though we use these examples to clarify the mystery of the Holy Trinity, we realize they are deficient in some way. Fortunately, what is required of us is acceptance of this mystery, and not understanding.

It is clear that Catholics believe in the mystery of the Holy Trinity, not because they understand it, but because they take the word of God for it. We often take the word of another for something we do not understand. For example, when we see a stone lying on the ground, it appears perfectly inactive. Yet physicists tell us that in reality the stone is a beehive of activity, for the smallest particles of that stone, its atoms and molecules, are quite active. How there can be activity in a stone is a mystery to us, but we are willing to believe what the physicists tell us, because we regard them as knowledgeable individuals.

It's much the same with respect to the Holy Trinity. We do not — indeed, we cannot — understand how there can be three distinct persons in the one God. However, we believe in the Holy Trinity because Almighty God has revealed this secret of his inner life through Jesus. We know that God is knowledge and truth; consequently, we believe whatever he tells us, whether we understand it or not.

It's good that we reflect on the mystery of the Holy Trinity from time to time. We need to remind ourselves occasionally how little we know about God after all. We read the Bible and it tells us many wonderful things about God and his relationship to the human race. On Sunday the preacher seems to speak so confidently about God and his ways. Yet reflection on the mystery of the Holy Trinity reminds us that we cannot fathom the depths of God's being. What we know about God is far less than what we do not know.

A final thought. When Our Lord revealed the mystery of the Holy Trinity, he also spoke of a divine Trinitarian presence in the believer. To those who love God, Jesus made a striking promise: "Whoever loves me will keep my word, and my Father will love him, and we will come to him and make our dwelling with him" (Jn 14:23). Furthermore, Jesus spoke of sending the Holy Spirit, the Advocate: "If I do not go, the Advocate will not come to you. But if I go, I will send him to you" (Jn 16:7).

In other words, Jesus promised the indwelling of the triune God in the believer who receives Christ's commandments and keeps them. Here is one of those core Christian truths which can make a real difference in our lives. It is not necessary to imagine or understand how the Holy Trinity dwells in the disciples of Christ. There need be no emotional response. What is wanted is the total conviction: the triune God is present and active in me. In that awareness I think and act and speak.

QUESTIONS FOR REVIEW

1. What is a mystery of the Christian religion?
2. What is the mystery of the Holy Trinity?
3. How did God reveal the mystery of the Holy Trinity?
4. How can we clarify to some extent the mystery of the Holy Trinity?
5. What is meant by the divine indwelling?

CHAPTER 3

CREATION

When we proclaim in the Apostles' Creed that God is the Creator of heaven and earth, we mean that he made all things from nothing by his almighty power. The question of the origin of the universe is such a basic one that it addresses itself to various disciplines — to archeology, astronomy, geology, paleontology, philosophy, and theology.

Each discipline must provide some answer in keeping with its own competence. The astronomer, for example, is concerned with the origin, constitution, and motion of celestial bodies. The paleontologist deals with the life of past geological periods as it can be known from fossil remains. The philosopher tries to answer the question about the origin of the universe by reflecting on the data provided by the other sciences, while the theologian tries to answer the question with the help of divine revelation.

We are presently concerned with the religious explanation of the origin of the universe. This explanation does not contradict nor render unnecessary the explanation that is proper to the other disciplines.

The Book of Genesis is the first book of the Bible. It was given this name because it is concerned with the origin of the world, of the human race, and, in particular, of the Hebrew people. Genesis opens with an account of creation (Gn 1:1-2:3). "In the beginning," the author wrote, "when God created the heavens and the earth, the earth was a formless wasteland, and darkness covered the abyss. . . ." (Gn 1:1-2). The author goes on to describe the works of creation in detail. For example, God separated the light from the darkness, and the land from the sea. He populated the sea with fish, and the land with animals; and finally he created man and woman in his own image. The works of creation were distributed over the course of six days, followed by a day of rest after the labor of creation.

By this account the author of Genesis was reacting against the myth of creation current among the Babylonians, the nation that held Israel captive from 587 till 537 B.C. According to this myth found in the epic known as *Enuma Elish*, there were two deities in the beginning, the male deity Apsu and the female deity Tiamat. These two deities were the parents of the gods. However, conflict broke out between the gods and their parents. Apsu was slain, and the gods enlisted the hero Marduk in their fight against Tiamat. Marduk engaged Tiamat in combat and slew her. From the gigantic carcass of Tiamat, Marduk created the visible universe: the earth resting upon the waters of the ocean, surmounted by the arch of the sky, above which are the chambers of rain and wind. Man was made of clay mixed with the blood of a slain god.

The author of Genesis wished to contradict this account of creation. To be sure, he incorporated certain elements of the Babylonian myth in his own account, but he disagreed with its fundamental ideas. The God of Genesis existed before, and is distinct from, all else. He did not engage other gods in combat in order to make the universe. God did not make the universe out of some preexisting matter. All things came into being at his word. For example, God said, "Let there be light," and there was light (Gn 1:3). No one assisted God in the work of creation. God is the absolute and serene master of all that he made. This is the meaning of the creation story in Genesis.

As the explanation of the origin of the universe, creation is not only proposed for our belief by the Book of Genesis, but it is also forced upon us by our reason. Creation is the act by which God made all things out of nothing. Whereas a carpenter makes a chair out of wood, God used no raw material to fashion the universe. There is no other way to explain the existence of the universe. God is an uncaused Being, infinite and unique. This was the conclusion of the very first talk of this series in which I discussed the existence of God and his attributes. All else has the characteristics of an effect, that is to say, of something dependent upon something else. All things besides God are finite, mutable, contingent, and multiple. Hence, prior to the act of creation only God existed; and when he produced beings other than himself, he had to make them out of nothing in the sense that there was no preexisting raw material.

Does the theory of evolution have a bearing upon this matter? The modern theory of evolution arose as the result of the work of the French botanist, Jean de Lamarck (1744-1829), and, more importantly, as the result of the work of Charles Darwin (1809-82), the English botanist and naturalist. In his *Origin of Species*, which was published in 1859, Darwin postulated that living forms result mainly from the variations occurring from generation to generation, usually gradually, but sometimes abruptly. Whereas forms unsuited to the environment tend to die out because they have a relatively poor chance of survival, those forms that do suit the environment tend to be perpetuated through individuals. This is the process of natural selection. In its scientific form, the theory of evolution offers a highly plausible explanation of *how* the universe developed; but it does not explain the origin of the universe in the first place.

Why did God create creatures in such extreme variety and numbers — from gnats to angels, we might ask. God did so to share his blessings with his creatures, for it is the nature of goodness to give. And each creature reflects in some way the nature of its Creator. Mountains reflect the eternity of God;

oceans, the depths of God's being. Men and women reflect the intelligence of God; and mothers and fathers, his love for his children.

One problem, though, troubles all thoughtful observers of God's creation. It is the problem of evil. Millions of human beings, children and adults, go hungry and even starve to death. Other millions are the victims of disease, war, exploitation, and deception. Still others perish in natural catastrophes, such as floods, earthquakes, and storms. If God is good, if he is all-powerful, if the world is subject to him as Lord, why does not God eliminate all evil? The question is easy to ask; but it is complicated to answer.

When we look at nature, we are almost convinced that some natural evils are quite necessary for nature to function. From time to time we go to a fast-food restaurant to enjoy a hamburger, but a cow had to be slaughtered to provide it. And the cow had to eat grass in order to develop.

Many evils are inflicted on the human race by wicked men and women. The corrupt ruler in a corrupt political system puts his rivals in prison and even murders them. Sometimes a criminal kills an innocent grocery clerk in the course of a robbery. The rapist does physical and emotional harm to his victim. The abuse of human freedom by wicked men and women is a terrible thing indeed. But the wisdom and justice of God are not defeated in dealing with it. God permits evil that good may come of it.

In some instances we can see the good that comes of evil. Perhaps in our own lives we can look back and see how bouts with illness or unemployment or some other evil have made us better persons for the experience. I have seen the members of a family drawn together by their concern for a sick child. I have seen the complete unselfishness of a son who cares for an invalid mother. I have seen the fidelity of a wife who stands by an alcoholic husband.

In many instances, however, we cannot see the good that comes of evil. Our vision of reality and our understanding of God's plans are too limited. There are many people who try to serve God faithfully. Yet they are cast in roles of suffering, and poverty, disease, or accident bring them to their graves. We must say that the spectacle of human suffering in these cases is scarcely intelligible apart from immortality. The Apostle Paul foresaw a happy ending to the tale of the Christian, one that does not occur in earthly days. He wrote to the Romans (8:18): "I consider that the sufferings of this present time are as nothing compared with the glory to be revealed for us." Our Savior himself died on a cross, but the meaning of his ignominious death was revealed by the resurrection that followed. Already in this life we share in the Savior's resurrection through our baptismal fellowship with him.

QUESTIONS FOR REVIEW

1. What is creation?
2. What does the Book of Genesis teach about the origin of the universe? Does modern science contradict this explanation?
3. What is the attitude of Catholics toward the theory of evolution?
4. Why does God allow evil to trouble his creation?

CHAPTER 4

MEN, WOMEN, AND ANGELS

Today I wish to speak to you about God's chief creatures, about men, women, and angels. Men and women are a composite of spiritual soul and material body. Angels are purely spiritual beings.

The author of the Book of Genesis, the first book of the Bible, gives two accounts of creation. In the first account (Gn 1:1-2:4a), the author sets forth the work of God in six days, followed by a sabbath of rest. Thereupon the author tells the story of creation a second time (Gn 2:4b-25). By this repetition, the author wished to teach his readers that men and women are superior to the other things created by God, being made in the divine image and likeness. In this second account of creation, it is the man who gives names to all the cattle, to the birds of the air, and to every beast of the field. This is the author's way of saying that the man is the lord of them all. The author of Genesis also wished to say that the woman shares in the dignity of the man. She is indeed bone of his bones and flesh of his flesh.

The Second Vatican Council appealed to these passages in Genesis and other books of the Bible to substantiate its own teaching about men and women. According to the Council, Scripture teaches that men and women were created in the image of God, that they are capable of knowing and loving their Creator, that they were appointed by him to be masters of all earthly creatures in order to subdue them and use them to

God's glory. Hence, all things should be related to men and women as their center and crown.

The Council went on to say that each individual is one person, even though he or she is composed of body and soul. The body is good and honorable, being a kind of microcosm of the material world. The soul is spiritual and immortal. By their intellects human beings surpass the material world. The intellect can know reality with certitude, and not only observable data. By their wills human beings are free and reflect the divine image in a remarkable way. Human dignity demands that men and women act knowingly and freely. They achieve their dignity when they pursue their end by a spontaneous choice of what is good and employ apt means to that end. This, I say, is the teaching of the Second Vatican Council about men and women, all of whom are made in the image and likeness of God.[1]

Still, the account of creation in the Book of Genesis does not have a happy ending. The man and woman were not content with their lot. The parents of the human race rebelled against their Maker (Gn 3). The result was that Adam and Eve were alienated from God. This alienation was accompanied by the deterioration of human nature itself in many important aspects including suffering and death (Rm 5:12) and concupiscence (Rm 13:14; Gal 5:17). Every infant born into the world is the victim of this alienation: he or she is infected with the sin of Adam (Rm 5:19) which is transmitted by propagation, and not by imitation. This sinful infection in each one of us is called original sin because it comes down to us through our origin or descent from Adam. Over the grave of each of us a stone could be erected with the inscription: "Here lies a man, the eldest son of sin and death."

I shall clarify the nature of original sin further when I speak about sanctifying grace and baptism.

1 Constitution on the Church in the Modern World, nos. 12-17.

I said a moment ago that the account of creation in the Book of Genesis does not have a happy ending. That is true. But the Book of Genesis does not tell the whole story. In the New Testament we have the prophetic fulfillment and completion of the story found in the third chapter of Genesis. The New Testament holds out the hope of reconciliation with the God of Genesis through the saving death of Jesus Christ. In a sense, Christ restores us to the garden of paradise where we walk in friendship with God once more. True, the members of this second Adam continue to struggle with concupiscence, temptation, suffering, and death; but the struggle is only temporary; the victory has been won.

However, I am getting ahead of myself. I shall return to the subject of Christ's saving death and his victory over sin on another occasion.

If men and women are by nature the crown of God's visible universe, angels are by nature the noblest of God's creatures. Angels are created spirits, without bodies, having intellect and free will.

Many modern thinkers deny the existence of angels. They have recast the old story in the Book of Genesis. There the angels with flaming swords banished the rebellious man and his wife from the garden of paradise (Gn 3:24). But today some thinkers have banished the angels from the world of creatures. They leave no room for angels no matter how economic the angels are with space. Angels, these thinkers say, are supposed to be immaterial; but these thinkers are familiar only with the material.

Some older ladies were traveling by auto on a lonely road. Suddenly they had a flat tire. The ladies stopped and got out of the car. One lady looked at the flat tire and said, "Only an angel from heaven can help us now." Then they heard a voice from above: "Just a moment. I'll come down and change the tire for you." It was the voice of a telephone lineman working above their heads. So, you see, there are angels after all.

We are familiar with the different ways in which angels are depicted in painting and sculpture. We have seen angels that look like infants with tiny wings; we have seen angels with puffed-out cheeks blowing trumpets; we have seen the angel Michael represented as a warrior doing battle with a serpent devil; we have seen the angel Gabriel represented as a chaste young man with long flowing hair. However, such pictures could be misleading. Angels are in fact beings superior to human beings. They are, as I have said, created spirits, without bodies, having understanding and free will.

Angels are frequently mentioned in the Bible.

According to the Old Testament, they exist in great numbers (Gn 32:1-3; Dn 7:10); they are members of the heavenly court (Is 6; Jb 1:6; 2:1); and they do God's will (Tb 12:18). In obedience to God's will, they communicate divine messages (Gn 31:11); they destroy and punish (2 K 19:35; 2 S 24:16); and they save and help (1 K 19:5-8).

According to the New Testament, Jesus himself accepted the popular belief in angels. For him, angels were spiritual beings (Mt 22:30); they constantly beheld the face of the heavenly Father (Mt 18:10); and they will accompany him at his second coming (Mt 16:27). Angels announce his conception (Mt 1:20) and his birth (Lk 2:9-15); they minister to him in the desert (Mt 4:11) and strengthen him in his agony (Lk 22:43); they are prepared to defend him when he is captured (Mt 26:53); and they are witnesses to his resurrection (Mt 28:2-7; Jn 20:12). Some angels have sinned (2 P 2:4; Jude 6). There are ranks and gradations among the angels (Lk 1:19; Ep 1:21; Jude 8-9). The worship of the angels in heaven is the model of the worship of the Church (Rv 4-5).

Just as we are persons, so the angels are persons too. Thus they are able to think and choose, just as we are. Angels differ from us, however, because they have no bodies. Sometimes, though, they take bodies to themselves in order to be seen by men and women.

Angels are creatures like us; God created them out of nothing. Almost immediately God imposed some manner of trial on the angels. Many angels remained faithful to God and, as a reward, they were admitted to the joys of heaven (Mt 18:10). Others, in their pride, did not remain faithful to God (2 P 2:4; Jude 6) and they were cast into hell for all eternity. Our Lord said that the everlasting fire of hell was prepared for the devil and his angels (Mt 25:41).

The angels were created primarily to know God and to love him. Yet the good angels render us many services. They are part of God's general plan whereby he cares for his creatures through other creatures. God's angels care for us (Ps 91:11-12). They direct, inspire, comfort, and encourage us (Tb 12:12-15). They are part of that gigantic conspiracy of kindness set on foot by Almighty God for our advantage.

Just as the good angels are able to help us, so too the demons or bad angels work against us (Ep 6:11; 1 P 5:8-9). This they do by tempting us to sin, although not all temptations come from the devil. Often temptations come from ourselves or from the world in which we live (Rm 7:22-23; 1 Jn 2:15). In rare cases God allows a demon to invade the body by a kind of possession, so that the body becomes a sort of instrument of the evil spirit (Mk 5:1-20).

QUESTIONS FOR REVIEW

1. What is the nature of human beings?
2. What is original sin?
3. What are angels?
4. What does the Bible tell us about angels?
5. How do the good angels help us?
6. How do the bad angels try to harm us?

CHAPTER 5

Jesus Christ (I)
WHO HE IS

God sent his only Son into the world to reconcile sinful men and women to himself. Let us speak today about him. For Catholics, Jesus Christ is the second person of the Blessed Trinity, true God and true man, the Savior of the world.

The Gospels are our most important source of information about the details of Jesus' life. The other writings of the New Testament recognize the centrality of Jesus; but they add no new details to those of the Gospels. The exact date of the birth of Jesus is unknown, but he must have lived between the death of Herod in 4 B.C. and the governorship of Pontius Pilate from A.D. 26 to 36. The public life of Jesus began among the poor of Galilee and ended in the city of Jerusalem. Jesus was addressed as "Rabbi" which means "Teacher," which indicates that he was regarded as one learned in the Jewish Law. The central theme of Jesus' preaching was the kingdom of God or the reign of God, an idea with deep roots in Jewish history.

Like any other rabbi, Jesus gathered disciples or followers around himself. They shared in his mission and were equipped with power to accomplish it. Despite considerable good will on their part, they were slow to grasp who Jesus was and what he was about. Finally, they came to recognize him as the Messiah, a leader whom the Jewish people had long awaited. By his association with sinners, by his critique of the religious law of his people, and by his manner of teaching with authority, Jesus provoked the opposition of almost every sect in contemporary society. He considered himself to be the last and greatest of the prophets. And he saw his own fate as a share in the cruel destiny of the rejected prophets. Jesus was executed by the Romans at the instigation of some of his own countrymen. The outcome of his passion and death was the resurrection.

I said at the beginning that Catholics believe Jesus Christ to be true God and true man. The Gospels make it quite clear that Jesus Christ was a true man. In other words, he had a human nature. He had a human body and a human soul with human intelligence, human freedom, and human emotions. He was born of the Virgin Mary; he developed from infancy through childhood and adolescence to adulthood; he was obedient to his parents; he was hungry, tired, and thirsty; he felt happiness and sadness; he experienced pain; and he died on a cross. He was like us in all things except sin.

Jesus Christ was not only true man, but also true God. He had not only a human nature, but also a divine nature. Jesus himself claimed to be God. This is the most natural explanation of the Church's faith in the divinity of Christ. Generally, Christ presented his claim in a veiled manner for teaching purposes, and his disciples did not understand the significance of his claim until after the illuminating experience of the resurrection, but there is evidence of the claim in the Gospels.

Jesus claimed the titles and prerogatives which the Jewish people associated with Yahweh, the God of Israel. Jesus spoke of his transcendent origin, so that his ancestor, David, knew him and called him Lord (Mk 12:35-37). Jesus claimed to be greater than Solomon, the prophets, and the temple (Mt 12:6, 41-42). Jesus claimed that the angels of heaven serve him (Mt 13:41; Mk 13:27). He is the only begotten Son who alone knows the Father and whose true nature is known by the Father alone (Mt 11:27; Lk 10:22). Jesus presented himself as the end-time king and judge (Mt 25:34-40). Jesus placed himself on a plane equal to God.

Still, when a person makes an important claim, he or she must substantiate that claim if others are to believe it. If we accepted every claim brought to our attention without seeking confirmation of it, we should be deceived over and over again. What proof did Jesus offer in support of his claim to be God?

The question was put to me quite forcefully some years ago. I spent a year in Japan studying the religions of the Far East. I also had the opportunity to travel throughout certain other countries on the continent of Asia. I saw for myself that the dominant religious figure in eastern Asia is the Buddha, which means the Enlightened One. The Buddha was a man who lived in India about five hundred years before the birth of Christ. One day, while sitting under a tree, he had a mystical experience. He came to the conclusion that the cause of suffering was desire, that the elimination of suffering could be achieved by suppressing desire. The Buddha traveled throughout northern India for the rest of his life teaching men and women what he had come to understand. He and his disciples won millions of converts. As I moved among the Buddhists of Asia, I had to ask myself, "Why have I committed myself to Christ rather than to the Buddha?"

I have also had the opportunity to travel in Moslem countries, such as Morocco, Turkey, Egypt, and parts of the Soviet Union in Central Asia. As you know, Moslems look upon Muhammad as the great prophet of God. Moslems honor Jesus, but they place Muhammad on a plane far above Jesus. As I traveled in these Moslem countries, I had to ask myself again, "Why am I a Christian rather than a Moslem?"

The answer to these questions lies, I believe, in the miraculous. We do not know Jesus at all, unless we know him as a wonder-worker. God has intervened in an extraordinary way in the life of Jesus. God has worked miracles through Jesus. God has guaranteed him to all by raising him from the dead. God has clearly identified Jesus as his spokesman, as his divine Son. As far as I can determine, there is no evidence of the miraculous in the life of the Buddha, or in the life of Muhammad, or in the lives of the founders of the other great religions of the world. I, for my part, am at peace about the truth of Jesus' claims.

So, then, Jesus was both God and man. The message of Jesus was the message of God in human words. In communicating his message to us, Jesus used words and images which were current among the Jewish people of his day. We must try to understand these words and images as well as we can, for they convey God's ideas to us. Whoever does not try to understand the words of Jesus and to act upon them is foolish indeed.

The central theme of Jesus' message to the world was the kingdom or reign of God, an idea current among the Jewish people of his day. They thought of God as a king who ruled the universe and guided the course of history. One day, they believed, God would intervene decisively in human history. He would eliminate the forces of evil opposing his rule, and God's people would share in that victory.

Jesus accepted this Jewish belief, but he clarified it. The kingdom or reign of God, he said, had already begun (Mk 1:15). The person and activity of Jesus were a sign of its presence. Jesus used many images to describe the expansion of God's kingdom. Just as a tiny seed becomes a large tree, so from an insignificant beginning God's rule will one day embrace all the nations of the world (Mk 4:30-32). Each time that we pray for the coming of the kingdom in the Lord's Prayer (Mt 6:10), we pray for the moment when the kingdom will attain its final growth and perfection.

What are the duties of individuals with respect to the kingdom or reign of God? The kingdom is essentially a gift (Mk 10:15; Lk 12:32), but at the same time it entails personal responsibility. Repentance and belief are the fundamental conditions for admittance into the kingdom (Mk 1:15). Repentance signifies a total transformation of one's being, a total conformity to the will of God, the cessation of sinful acts, and a revolution in one's point of view and desires, so that one becomes a new creature, as the parable of the prodigal son (Lk 15:11-32) and the parable of the Pharisee and tax-collector indicate (Lk 18:9-14).

In the light of these and other passages of the New Testament, we may say that the kingdom or reign of God is established when men and women do the will of God. A new and final phase of the reign of God began with the appearance of Jesus and his proclamation of the kingdom. During its earthly existence the kingdom is beset by opposition and evil, but the moment is coming when God will drive out all that is contrary, and the kingdom will achieve its complete fulfillment.

QUESTIONS FOR REVIEW

1. Who is Jesus Christ?
2. What are some of the main details of Jesus' life?
3. What is the evidence for his humanity?
4. How did Jesus claim divinity?
5. How did Jesus support his claim to divinity?
6. What is the kingdom or reign of God?

CHAPTER 6

Jesus Christ (II)
THE HIDDEN YEARS

The Gospels of Matthew (1:18) and Luke (1:35) state that Jesus was conceived by his mother Mary in a virginal manner. That is to say, Mary conceived her Son through the overshadowing of the Holy Spirit without the intervention of a man. Some interpreters of the Gospels believe that this statement is not to be taken literally, that it is only an image of the truth that Jesus was God's Son from the beginning. Other interpreters of the Gospels believe that the virginal conception of Jesus is to be taken literally because it is difficult to explain how the early Christians happened upon the idea of a virginal conception — unless, of course, that is what really occurred. A binding teaching of the Catholic Church affirms the virginal conception of Jesus in a literal sense.

We may ask why God chose to become a human being in this extraordinary manner. The reason is not hard to discover. The incarnation of the Son of God marked a new beginning. Just as the first Adam, the parent of the human race, had no earthly father, so Jesus Christ, the second Adam, the parent of a new race of redeemed individuals, had no earthly father.

The Gospel of Luke (2:7) describes the rough simplicity of the Savior's birth after his virginal conception. We might have expected the Son of God to be born in a palace or mansion. The commentator, William Barclay, tells the story of a European king who worried his court by disappearing often and walking incognito among his people. He was asked not to do so for the sake of security. But he answered: "I cannot rule my people unless I know how they live." It is a great truth of the Christian religion that God has lived among us. He knows how we live. He claimed no special advantage over common men and women.

By being born of Mary and living among us, the incarnate Son of God gave us a pattern of conduct. We could not imitate the all-holy God whom we could not see, nor should we imitate the sinful men and women whom we could see. So God became man that we might have a model of conduct. God in the flesh is a brother in the flesh. He is an inspiration to us in the vicissitudes of life. He teaches us how to turn them to good account. He enables us to view them in the right perspective. As often as we walk and talk and breathe, as often as we ache and grow tired and grieve, we are comforted by the thought that Our Blessed Lord did just that, that he felt just as we do.

Eight days after his birth, the child Jesus was circumcised (Lk 2:21). Circumcision is, of course, a kind of surgical operation. For many who practice it, it has no religious significance. For the Jews of Our Lord's day, it did have a religious significance: it was a token of membership in God's people and of association with the covenant. Generally, it was the father who performed the operation. Later a surgeon did it. At the ceremony a name was given the child. When Our Lord was circumcised, by the command of God he was given the name Jesus, which means Savior, because he was to save his people from their sins (Lk 2:21; Mt 1:21). Why was Jesus circumcised? For a variety of reasons, among them, to demonstrate the reality of his human nature and to dramatize his Jewish heritage.

The Gospel of Matthew speaks of the visit of the Magi or

astrologers to the child Jesus at Bethlehem (2:1-12). This visit is recalled on the feast of the Epiphany. The word, epiphany, is derived from a Greek word which means "manifestation." The feast of the Epiphany celebrates the manifestation of the Savior to the entire human race. Just as Jesus manifested himself to the Jewish shepherds on Christmas day, so he manifested himself to the Gentile Magi on the Epiphany.

Some commentators on the Gospel of Matthew think that the story of the Magi or astrologers is only a lovely legend. Perhaps! I note only that there were men like the Magi in the ancient world. They did believe in astrology. When Jesus was born, there was a general expectation of a new king. The visit of the Magi was exactly the kind of thing that could have happened in those days.

By telling the story of the Magi Matthew revealed the openness of Jesus to all men and women, Jew and Gentile alike. It is true that at the outset of his public life Jesus and his disciples preached only to the Jewish nation (Mt 10:6; 15:24). Nevertheless, Jesus acknowledged that he had been sent to lay down his life for all men and women (Mk 14:24). He anticipated the gathering of his elect from the four winds (Mt 8:11). At the close of his life on this earth Jesus sent his representatives to preach to all nations and generations (Mt 28:19). Jesus was convinced that God was the Father of all.

If Jesus was characterized by openness to all, his followers should also be. We cannot close our hearts to anyone, whether he or she be white, black, yellow, or brown. If we are going to imitate Our Savior, our hearts have to be open to human beings in all strata of society in every corner of the earth.

Finally, I should like to say a word about those hidden years which Jesus spent at Nazareth. During those thirty years Jesus grew from an infant to an adult. What was Jesus doing during those silent years at Nazareth?

First, Jesus was growing up in a good home. The Gospel of Luke tells us that the Holy Family of Jesus, Mary, and Joseph made their home at Nazareth. There Jesus was obedient to his parents and advanced in wisdom and age and favor before God and man (Lk 2:51-52). All Christians have in the Holy Family an example of, and an invitation to, the practice of every Christian virtue. At the end of the nineteenth century, Pope Leo XIII remarked that those who have an abundance of this world's goods ought to learn from the Holy Family that a good life is better than riches, while all those who find themselves in a humble station of life will have cause for joy rather than sorrow, if they consider the Holy Family. In common with the Holy Family they too are distressed by the labors and cares of daily life.

Secondly, during those silent years at Nazareth, Jesus was working in the carpenter shop of his foster-father Joseph. It seems that Joseph died while Jesus was still a young man at Nazareth. Joseph was not present at the marriage feast of Cana (Jn 2:1-11), although Jesus and Mary were present. So Jesus became the carpenter of Nazareth to support his mother and himself. If we could have visited his shop, probably we would have seen some very primitive equipment: one or two saws, a hatchet, a hammer, a mallet, a plane, and perhaps a workbench or sawhorse. These tools were sufficient for making the usual things: doors, window frames, chests for wardrobes, yokes for oxen, and plows for the field. Occasionally, a carpenter was called upon to square off roughly the beams of poplar and sycamore that were used to support the thatched roof of a house under construction.

It is difficult to exaggerate the dignity of work. Jesus himself baptized it by the sweat of his brow. Work is the activity of a human being made in the image and likeness of God. By their work men and women make life on this earth more human and achieve their eternal destiny. By their work men and women support their families and serve other human beings. They become partners with God in developing his creation. When people work, they develop themselves as well. They learn much, they cultivate their resources, they go outside themselves and beyond themselves. This kind of growth is of greater value than any external riches. A person is more precious for what he or she is than for anything he or she might possess. I grieve when I hear about the unemployed. Not only do the unemployed suffer financially, but they are deprived of the work by which they develop themselves as persons.

Finally, during those silent years at Nazareth, Jesus was preparing himself for his public ministry. He communed with his heavenly Father in prayer. He did the will of his heavenly Father as that will was revealed in the events of his daily life. He learned to understand the life of ordinary people. He learned fidelity in small things. He teaches us the importance of preparation for the success of any enterprise.

QUESTIONS FOR REVIEW

1. How was Jesus conceived?
2. How is the incarnate Son of God a pattern of conduct?
3. Why was Jesus circumcised?
4. What is the meaning of the Magi's visit?
5. What was Jesus doing during the hidden years at Nazareth?
6. How important is work?

CHAPTER 7

Jesus Christ (III)
HIS PASSION AND DEATH

What does the death of Christ on Calvary mean to Catholics? The answer is that it was a sacrificial death by which he reconciled us to our heavenly Father, who had been alienated from the human race by sin. Allow me to explain.

We have to understand the significance of Christ's death on the cross against the background of human sinfulness. Sin took hold of the human race long before the death of Christ on Calvary. At the very beginning of human history, shrouded in obscurity as it is, the parents of the human race rebelled against their Maker. The result was that Adam and Eve and their descendants were estranged or alienated from God.

This alienation was accompanied by the deterioration of human nature itself in many important respects, including concupiscence, suffering, and death. Every infant born into the world is the victim of this alienation: he or she is infected with the sin of Adam which is transmitted by propagation, and not by imitation. This sinful infection in each one of us is called original sin. In somewhat similar fashion, a child can inherit a physical disease from its parents.

However, original sin and its consequences are only the beginning of the sad situation. Each one of us adds to the heavy burden of sin inherited from our first parents. We commit actual sins. We do not make God the center of our lives; we are indifferent to the needs of others and even injure them; we pursue selfish pleasure in the face of all that is reasonable. In effect, we shake our fists in the face of our Father in heaven and withdraw our loyalty and friendship. We say with the demons, "I will not serve."

How did God choose to cope with human sinfulness? What is a loving Father to do when his children turn against him? How does he win them back without compromising their precious gift of freedom? In order to answer these questions, let us consider three possibilities. I am indebted to St. Thomas Aquinas (*ca* 1225-74), one of the Church's greatest theologians, for recognizing these possibilities and evaluating them in the light of the New Testament.[1]

The first possibility was this: To deal with human sinfulness, God could simply have pardoned his repentant sons and daughters without making any further demands upon them. But God did not choose to implement this first possibility because it did not fully reveal the depth of God's love for us and the horror of sin.

Then there was a second possibility: God could have demanded satisfaction for sin without willing the death of his divine Son. The Son of God could have assumed a human nature and offered infinite satisfaction to God by every action, by every prayer, by every word. But God did not choose to implement this second possibility either, because it too did not fully reveal the depth of God's love for his children and the horror of sin.

So God chose to implement a third possibility: the way of sacrifice and satisfaction, the way of suffering and death. To win back his sinful sons and daughters, God chose to overwhelm them with proof of his love. Out of overflowing love God

1 *Summa Theologiae* 3a.46.1-3.

willed the death of his sinless Son as a sacrifice and satisfaction for sin. Out of the same great love the Son of God freely accepted the decree of his Father. "No one has greater love than this," Jesus said, "to lay down one's life for one's friends" (Jn 15:13). And what is even more, Jesus laid down his life for sinners, who are not the friends of God, but hostile to him. As Paul wrote in his letter to the Christians at Rome, "God proves his love for us in that while we were still sinners Christ died for us" (Rm 5:8).

We wonder at the love, wisdom, and power at work in God's plan of salvation. Could God have chosen a more effective way to win back his sinful sons and daughters without compromising their freedom? In the face of God's love, can sinful human beings remain indifferent? Must not a child run to its father's open arms? Must not ice melt before the flame? Must not a flower open to the sun?

After weighing all these considerations, St. Thomas Aquinas drew this conclusion: "Through the passion and death of Christ, we sinners know how much God loves us, and we are stirred to love him in return; and herein lies our salvation."[2]

The theme of Christ's sacrificial death on Calvary is intimated already in the Old Testament. In the Book of Isaiah, for example, we read the great messianic oracles known as the Songs of the Servant of the Lord. Isaiah speaks of a mysterious Servant of the Lord who, he said,

> Was pierced for our offenses, crushed for our sins,
> Upon him was the chastisement that makes us whole,
> By his stripes we were healed.
>
> We had all gone astray like sheep,
> Each following his own way;
> But the LORD laid upon him the guilt of us all.

2 *ibid.*, 3a.46.3.

Though he was harshly treated, he submitted
And opened not his mouth;
Like a lamb led to the slaughter
Or a sheep before the shearers,
He was silent and opened not his mouth. . . .

When he was cut off from the land of the living,
And smitten for the sin of his people,
A grave was assigned him among the wicked
And a burial place with evildoers,
Though he had done no wrong nor spoken any falsehood. . . .

He surrendered himself to death
And was counted among the wicked;
And he shall take away the sins of many
And win pardon for their offenses. (Is 53:5-12)

It is not certain who the Suffering Servant of the Lord was in the mind of Isaiah. Commentators have identified the Servant with the nation of Israel or with some historical character or even with the prophet himself; but the New Testament and Christian tradition have seen the fulfillment of Isaiah's words in Jesus Christ.

The theme of Christ's sacrificial death on Calvary recurs over and over again in the pages of the New Testament. It is impossible to cite all the variations of the theme composed by the inspired authors, but I shall mention a few. In the Gospel of Mark, we hear Jesus say, "The Son of Man did not come to be served but to serve and to give his life as a ransom for many" (Mk 10:45). Then, at the solemn moment when Our Lord gave us the Holy Eucharist, Jesus explained the significance of his passion and death in the same vein. During the meal he spoke of his own blood as "the blood of the covenant, which will be shed on behalf of many for the forgiveness of sins" (Mt 26:28). According to Paul, Christ made peace between God and man through the blood of his cross (Col 1:20). The witness of the New Testament is unanimous: Christ sacrificed his life for sinners in obedience to his heavenly Father.

I once read a story about two men who were part of a crew repairing a railroad bridge. The job of one man was to stand on the tracks and lower his partner to a platform below the bridge. As this man was standing on the tracks, lowering his friend, a coal car, which had broken away from its train, began to roll toward him. The man on the tracks did not panic. He let the rope down carefully until his friend reached the platform below the bridge. Just as he did, the runaway car struck the man on the tracks, and he was killed instantly. He had given his life to save his friend.

In a similar way, Jesus sacrificed his life to save us from the second death, that is to say, separation from our Father in heaven and all that implies. The great task of the present life is to unite ourselves ever more closely to the death of Christ on Calvary. How? "Repent and believe in the gospel," Jesus said at the beginning of his public ministry (Mk 1:15). If you love the Lord your God with your whole heart and your neighbor as yourself, Jesus told the lawyer, you shall live (Lk 10:25-28). Union with the death of Christ on Calvary is the great enterprise of the present life.

We Catholics display the crucifix so prominently in our homes to remind us of the fateful events of Calvary. Indeed, the whole world reminds us of Christ and his passion and death. As Joseph Mary Plunkett (1887-1916), the Irish poet wrote:

> I see his blood upon the rose
> And in the stars the glory of his eyes,
> His body gleams amid eternal snows,
> His tears fall from the skies.

I see his face in every flower;
The thunder and singing of the birds
Are but his voice — and carven by his power
Rocks are his written words.

All pathways by his feet are worn,
His strong heart stirs the ever-beating sea.
His crown of thorns is twined with every thorn,
His cross is every tree.

QUESTIONS FOR REVIEW

1. How did God choose to bring sinners back to himself?
2. What does the Bible teach about the death of Christ?
3. How do we unite ourselves to, or share the benefits of, Christ's death on Calvary?

CHAPTER 8

JESUS CHRIST (IV)
HIS RESURRECTION AND ASCENSION

Having spoken to you about the death of Christ on Calvary and its significance for Catholics, I now wish to speak to you about the resurrection of Christ from the dead and his ascension into heaven. The death and resurrection of Christ are the central events of his life, and our redemption was not complete until Christ had risen from the dead. His ascension into heaven brought his life on this earth to a close.

I used the word, redemption, just now. By the redemption I mean that God forgives the sins of men and women because Jesus Christ made satisfaction to God in our stead and for us by his sacrificial death on the cross. Still, as I have said, our redemption was not complete until Jesus rose from the dead. For example, Paul wrote that Jesus "was handed over for our transgressions and was raised for our justification" (Rm 4:25).

Some years ago, the English author, Graham Greene, wrote a spy novel called *The Human Factor.* In the course of the novel, the principal character, a man named Castle, explained his difficulties with Christianity. Such things as a virgin birth, miracles, and resurrection from the dead were simply incredible for him.

Surely the bald assertion that someone has risen from the dead is for many absolutely incredible. One recalls the reaction of certain Greeks to Paul's preaching in Athens. After Paul had spoken of Jesus' resurrection from the dead, "some began to scoff" (Ac 17:32). Yet the assertion that *Jesus* rose from the dead becomes less incredible if one is prepared to grant certain possibilities: that the human race could have benefited by a message from God; that God could have imparted this message through agents; that the profoundly religious figure, Jesus of Nazareth, could have been an agent of God; that God could have guaranteed him to all by raising him from the dead.

Indeed, the rise of the Christian Church supposes the reality of Jesus' resurrection. Despite Jesus' ignominious death on the cross, despite the severe psychological blow of Jesus' crucifixion, the apostles of Jesus and the Christian Church began to proclaim Jesus as God and Savior. Could they have done so if Jesus' body had remained in the tomb?

The resurrection was more than the restoration of the slain Jesus to the conditions of the present life; rather, it conferred on him a new and permanent form of life in glory and power. The New Testament does not describe the actual event of the resurrection. It tells only of the empty tomb and the appearances of the risen Jesus to his disciples. According to the accounts, the resurrected Jesus was able to pass through closed doors; and he appeared and disappeared with an unnatural suddenness. His appearances to his followers caused them to fear and doubt his reality at first, yet he was not a phantom. The Gospel of Luke tells us that the Risen Lord asked his disciples for something to eat. They put before him a piece of cooked fish which he took and ate in their presence (Lk 24:41-43). We can easily picture the cheerful Risen Savior removing a small fish bone from his mouth. The friends of Jesus could see and touch him. Those who saw him recognized him as their former master who had been crucified. After his resurrection Jesus enjoyed a glorious, spiritual existence, freed from the possibility of decline and death. Hence Christianity is not primarily a philosophical system or an ethical movement. It is a religion in a very concrete and realistic sense because it rests on a fact: Jesus rose from the dead.

The resurrection of Jesus is a cause of great joy for Christians for several reasons. First, the resurrection was the victory of Christ over death with results not only for himself, but for all Christians. In virtue of the death and resurrection of Christ we, who follow Christ into death, will rise after him. Paul, especially, is emphatic on this point. In his Letter to the Romans, he expressed his conviction that the effect of baptism is to conform us here and now to the Risen Christ. Just as Christ rose from the dead to a new life, so the baptized Christian begins to live a new life. Paul goes on to say that this present renewal is the prelude to the Christian's bodily resurrection and admission to eternal life (Rm 6:1-11).

In his Second Letter to the Corinthians, Paul wrote that "the one who raised the Lord Jesus will raise us also with Jesus and place us with you in his presence" (2 Cor 4:14). Certainly our divine Savior has not eliminated death from the scheme of things. You and I shall indeed die, but we shall live forever afterwards. And so we Christians rejoice. We rejoice in the victory of Our Lord over death; we rejoice in the promise of immortality that the resurrection of Jesus guarantees us. As a result, for the believing Christian the worst and last of life's horrors turns out to be a harmless bogey.

The resurrection of Jesus is a cause of great joy for a second reason. Christ is not only risen and living, but he is living and present. If we read the Acts of the Apostles, that book of the New Testament which describes the first days of the Christian community, we are struck with the prevailing mood of joy. Why? Because the first Christians entertained the deepest and most vivid conviction that Christ was invisibly, but truly present among them. We should do well to cultivate in our lives an awareness of the literal, dynamic presence of the Risen Christ.

Such an awareness can make new men and women of us, just as it did for the original apostles and disciples. I once read about a minister who was working on his sermon for Easter. As he pondered the resurrection, quite suddenly its meaning dawned on him more clearly than ever before. He rose from his chair and began to pace the floor of his study. "Christ is alive," he said to himself; and he repeated the word "alive" over and over again. "He is living, just as I am living." And he began to say over and over again: "He is living, just as I am living." The minister had believed in the resurrection of Christ as long as he could remember, but now he began to appreciate its meaning more fully. Do we really appreciate the fact that Christ is alive, that he is living, just as we are living?

Awareness of the Risen Christ means victory over trouble and disaster. It is able to keep a person from being defeated by the disappointments and frustrations of daily life. Awareness of the living Christ also means victory over fear. It produces a serenity of mind and spirit which is much more powerful than fear. Men and women of faith will be buffeted by life's storms no less than their neighbors. But by virtue of their relationship to the Risen Christ, there is nothing either in life or death that need finally defeat them.

The resurrection of Jesus is a cause of joy for a third reason. Christ risen and victorious will come again. Each one of us is moving steadily toward a personal encounter with Christ. The first Christians knew, and we know, that the Risen Christ will return. He will return to judge — to judge mercifully, lovingly, Savior-like. In his lifetime Christ promised reward much more than punishment.

The ascension of Jesus means that he was taken to heaven, body and soul, in the glorified state which he enjoyed after his resurrection. The ascension marks the completion of his work on this earth and his departure from the corporeal universe.

Actually, the New Testament speaks of the ascension of Jesus in two ways. First, there are texts which affirm the exaltation of Jesus in heaven without mentioning his being taken up explicitly. For example, on the occasion of his martyrdom, Stephen told his persecutors: "Behold, I see the heavens opened and the Son of Man [Jesus] standing at the right hand of God" (Ac 7:56). Such a text and others like it suppose the glorification of Jesus in heaven and his previous departure from the corporeal universe by his ascension.

Second, there are texts in the New Testament which represent the ascension of Jesus as an established historical fact observable by sensible experience. Such texts appear only in the Gospel of Luke and the Acts of the Apostles. For example, we read: "Then he [Jesus] led them [his disciples] [out] as far as Bethany, raised his hands, and blessed them. As he blessed them he parted from them and was taken up to heaven" (Lk 24:50-51).

Despite the physical details of these scenes we must say that the ascension is primarily the exaltation and glorification of Jesus after the humiliation of his passion and death. "The ascension is the sign and seal of the ultimate accomplishment of his mission."[1]

1 John McKenzie, S.J., *Dictionary of the Bible* (Milwaukee: Bruce Pub. Co., 1965), "Ascension."

QUESTIONS FOR REVIEW

1. Why do Christians say that Jesus rose from the dead?
2. Was Jesus different before and after his resurrection?
3. Why is the resurrection a cause of joy for Christians?
4. What is the meaning of Jesus' ascension into heaven?

CHAPTER 9

THE HOLY SPIRIT

Just before he left this earth, Jesus told his apostles not to leave Jerusalem. Rather, they should "wait for the promise of the Father," he told them. And then he went on to say, "John baptized with water, but in a few days you will be baptized with the Holy Spirit" (Ac 1:4-5). This promise was fulfilled on Pentecost Sunday when the Holy Spirit descended upon the apostles and others with the appearance of tongues of fire. It is about the Holy Spirit that I wish to speak to you now.

Do we not feel somewhat guilty when we think about the Holy Spirit? Do we think about the Spirit as often as we should? Do we not neglect the Spirit in our devotions? To some degree this neglect is understandable. We cannot form a picture of the Spirit as easily as we can form a picture of Jesus. We can easily imagine the Infant Savior lying in the crib. We can picture Jesus asleep in the boat or speaking to the crowds or hanging on the cross. But we can form no such picture of the Holy Spirit. Yet, the Holy Spirit is God, a person like the Father and the Son, equal in every respect to them. With the Father and the Son he is worshiped and glorified, as we testify every Sunday in the creed of the Mass.

The New Testament attributes an important role to the Holy Spirit in the life of the faithful. At the conclusion of his earthly ministry, Jesus commanded his representatives to "make disciples of all nations, baptizing them in the name of the Father, and of the Son, and of the Holy Spirit" (Mt 28:19). In the Acts of the Apostles, the Holy Spirit is often characterized as a dynamic force, which moves the apostles to preach and give witness to Jesus, and empowers them to feats of courage and eloquence which are beyond their normal strength. For example, we are told that on the first Christian Pentecost "all were filled with the Holy Spirit and began to speak in different tongues, as the Spirit enabled them to proclaim" (Ac 2:4). According to the Acts of the Apostles, the Holy Spirit is given not only to the leaders of the Church, but also to the entire body of believers.

In his Second Letter to the Corinthians, Paul wishes his readers the abiding presence of the Holy Spirit. He writes: "The grace of the Lord Jesus Christ and the love of God and the fellowship of the Holy Spirit be with all of you" (2 Cor 13:13). You will recall that the priest addresses his people with these words at the beginning of Mass.

The personality and role of the Holy Spirit are clearly revealed in the Gospel of John. The Spirit is the Paraclete (Helper), the Spirit of truth (Jn 14:17; 15:26), who dwells in the apostles (Jn 14:17). The world does not know the Spirit (Jn 14:17), who is sent by the Father and Jesus (Jn 14:26; 15:26). The Spirit teaches (Jn 14:26) and witnesses (Jn 15:26) and convicts the world of sin (Jn 16:8-11). The Spirit does not speak of himself (Jn 16:13); he comes after Jesus (Jn 16:7) and reveals his true teaching (Jn 14:26; 16:13). The Spirit remains forever (Jn 14:16). According to the Gospel of John, the Spirit or Paraclete shares his functions with Jesus; but there is a distinction between the two. The Paraclete is to the continuing life of the Church what Jesus was to its foundation.

I am reminded of an experience out of my boyhood when my mother went to the hospital to have a baby. My father had to go to work every day, so he could not stay with us children. So my mother's sister came to live with us for several days. She cooked for us and cleaned the house and washed our clothes. She talked with us and prayed with us. In other words, she took my mother's place.

When Jesus spoke of sending the Holy Spirit, the Paraclete, he said in effect: "I am going back to my Father in heaven. You won't see me any more. But I am not going to leave you alone. I am going to send the Holy Spirit, who will remain with you and take care of you." The Holy Spirit takes the place of Jesus for the time being, just as my aunt took my mother's place during her absence. True, we cannot see or touch or hear the Holy Spirit. But the promise of Christ to send the Spirit is enough to reassure us of the reality of the gift.

We speak of the Holy Spirit as the Paraclete, the Helper; and we may speak of him as the soul of the Church, the Christian community. What the soul is to the body, that the Holy Spirit is to the Church, the body of Christians. Paul especially likes to speak of the Church as the body of Christ. He is comparing the Church to a human body. The human body has different members — the eye, the ear, the foot, and so on — each of which has a different function which it exercises for the benefit of the whole body. In the same way, the Church has different members with different functions (Rm 12:3-8; 1 Cor 12:12-31).

Among its members, the Church counts laity and clergy. The responsibility of the laity is to live the gospel in the specific situation in which they find themselves, whether they be mothers and fathers, factory workers, professional persons, students, or something else. The responsibility of the clergy is to shepherd the flock of Christ. If all of us members of the Church meet our personal responsibility, we contribute to the welfare of the whole Church. If we neglect our responsibility, the whole Church suffers. In this sense, the Church is a body whose members have different gifts and functions. In Paul's view, these vital gifts and functions are derived from the Holy Spirit (1 Cor 12:4-11, 27-31). Therefore, we may speak of the

Holy Spirit as the soul of the Church, since a body derives its vital functions from the soul.

The Acts of the Apostles tells us about the marvelous transformation that took place in the hearts of the apostles after the Spirit descended upon them. At first they were timid and fearful; but after the descent of the Spirit, they boldly professed Christ to the assembled multitudes (Ac 2:1-4). It is the teaching of the Catholic Church that through the sacrament of confirmation a baptized person receives the same special grace which the apostles received on Pentecost; that is to say, the grace to profess Christ boldly by word and deed. Each member of the Church, the body of Christ, will utilize that grace in the particular circumstances in which he or she is situated.

All of which brings us to the question: How can I make the influence of the Holy Spirit more effective in my life? How can I become more attuned to the promptings of the Holy Spirit?

One way is to lead a virtuous life. A virtuous person is sensitive to the voice of the Holy Spirit, just as a conductor is sensitive to the sounds of his orchestra. The chaste person, for example, will recognize the voice of the Holy Spirit in matters of chastity, while the unchaste person will be deaf to it. A virtuous life creates a capacity to resonate with the promptings of the Holy Spirit.

A second way is to exclude those voices which drown out the voice of the Spirit, such as excessive concern for material possessions, voices raised in quarrels, worry about the future, bitter criticism of others, worldly books and magazines. Some things which drown out the voice of the Spirit are good in themselves; but when we are occupied with them, we are not thinking about the things of God. Often it is the second best in our lives that is the worst enemy of the best.

Finally, we must pray for the guidance of the Spirit. When parents are perplexed about the needs of their children, let them pray to the Holy Spirit. When young people wish to discover their vocation in life or when they are seeking a suitable partner for marriage, let them pray to the Holy Spirit. When single persons seek to go it alone, let them pray to the Holy Spirit. The Spirit will respond!

QUESTIONS FOR REVIEW

1. Who is the Holy Spirit?
2. What is the role of the Holy Spirit in the life of the Church?
3. In what sense is the Holy Spirit the soul of the Church?
4. What is the connection between the Holy Spirit and confirmation?
5. How can we become more responsive to the Holy Spirit?

CHAPTER 10

The Blessed Virgin Mary (I)
THE MOTHER OF GOD

Having spoken about God, I should like to speak about Mary, the Mother of God. According to Catholic teaching, Mary is the most highly favored of God's creatures after the humanity of Christ.

One of my earliest recollections about the Church's teaching on Mary stems from my grade school days. One day our teacher asked, "Who was the greatest person who ever lived on this earth?" We all knew the answer: "Jesus Christ." Then she asked, "Why?" Again we all knew the answer: "Because he was God."

Then she asked, "Who was the greatest person after Jesus Christ?" This time we weren't sure. One boy suggested that Christopher Columbus was, because he had discovered America. A girl thought that George Washington was, because he was the father of his country. Another girl thought that Franklin Roosevelt was, because her daddy had said so. But none of these answers satisfied the teacher.

Finally, she said that Mary, the mother of Jesus, was greater than any of those whom we had mentioned. True, she had never discovered a new continent as Columbus had done. She had never been president of her country. But Mary was the Mother of God. She had obeyed God perfectly in all things. She had never sinned. She had loved God with her whole heart and soul, and she had loved others as she loved herself. Our teacher's answer reflected the teaching of the Catholic Church about Mary, the mother of Jesus.

Mary (or Miriam) was the name of the sister of Moses, the great leader of the Hebrew people. It was the name of several women in the New Testament; and it was the name of the mother of Jesus, the wife of Joseph. The Gospel of Matthew speaks of Mary in connection with the birth of Jesus, the visit of the Magi, and the flight into Egypt. The Gospel of Luke speaks of Mary in connection with the annunciation, the visit of Mary to her cousin Elizabeth, the birth of Jesus, his presentation in the temple, and losing and finding him in the temple. Luke portrays Mary as a pious Jewish woman obedient to the Law.

Mary appears in the Gospels of Matthew and Mark as one well-known to the people of Nazareth; and in the Gospels of Matthew, Mark, and Luke, Mary and the kinsmen of Jesus come to visit him during his public ministry. John speaks of Mary in connection with the marriage feast of Cana; he records her presence at the foot of the cross; and he tells how the crucified Jesus committed his mother to the care of the beloved disciple. The New Testament is silent about the further course of her life and death. The relatively minor role which Mary plays in the Gospels reflects the generally minor role of women in Jewish life.

There are several reasons why Catholics esteem Mary, the mother of Jesus, so highly. First of all, she is responsible for our salvation in a very real sense. Luke records the conversation between the messenger of God and the virgin of Nazareth (Lk 1:26-38). In effect the angel said to Mary: "Mary, do you consent to become the mother of God's Son, the One who will save his people?" In reply, Mary said: "Yes, I consent to become the mother of God's Son, the Savior of the world." With Mary's consent, the whole process of human salvation was set in motion. When God asked for Mary's consent, he did not play games. There was a causal relationship between Mary's consent and our salvation. This is one of the reasons why Catholics honor Mary so highly.

There is a second reason. The first chapter of Luke's Gospel tells how the angel Gabriel addressed Mary for the first time. The angel said: "Hail, favored one! The Lord is with you" (Lk 1:28). Luke also records the words of Mary's cousin Elizabeth, when Mary went to visit her. Elizabeth was filled with the Holy Spirit and cried out in a loud voice: "Most blessed are you among women, and blessed is the fruit of your womb. . . . Blessed are you who believed that what was spoken to you by the Lord would be fulfilled" (Lk 1:42, 45). In the *Magnificat*, that is to say, in Mary's canticle of praise, she appears totally at the service of God and his people. Hence, Mary foretells that "from now on will all ages call me blessed" (Lk 1:48). The praise of Mary in the first chapter of Luke's Gospel resounds in the hearts and on the lips of all Catholics. They too wish to be among those of all ages who call her blessed. This is a second reason why Catholics honor Mary so highly.

There is a third reason. She is the Mother of God. Indeed, this is the basis of her greatness and the reason for the favors conferred on her by the Almighty. Matthew and John speak of Mary as the mother of Jesus (Mt 1:18; Jn 19:25) and Luke speaks of Mary as the mother of the Lord (Lk 1:43). However, Mary is rightly called the Mother of God. The relationship between a mother and her son is a personal relationship, and Mary's Son is a divine person; therefore, Mary is truly the Mother of God. Just as human parents are truly the parents of their children even though the children derive only their bodies and not their souls from them, so Mary is the Mother of God even though her divine Son derived only his humanity and not his divinity from her.

The Gospels of Matthew and Luke speak explicitly of the virginal conception of Jesus. Without the intervention of a man, Mary became the mother of Jesus through the overshadowing of the Holy Spirit (Mt 1:18; Lk 1:34). This is the faith which the Catholic Church has professed from the beginning. We may ask why the Son of God chose to become man in this extraordinary manner. The reason is not difficult to discover. The incarnation of the Son of God marked a new beginning. Just as the first Adam, the parent of the human race, had no earthly father, so Jesus Christ, the new Adam, the last Adam, the parent of a new race of redeemed individuals, had no earthly father.

Was Mary the mother of children other than Jesus? The Catholic Church does not believe so. Mary was ever a virgin because of the utter devotion of her whole being and life to the pure service of God and Christ (1 Cor 7:34). The early Church thought that Mary must surely have been content with the divine Son God gave her. Against this background we understand why Jesus, dying on the cross, entrusted his mother to the care of a disciple and not to another son (Jn 19:25-27). Still, there are references in the Gospels to brothers and sisters of Jesus which suggest that Mary had children other than Jesus. See, for example, Mark 6:3. However, references to brothers and sisters can refer in the Semitic world to close relatives and relations by marriage. Catholics understand the Gospel references in this sense. But the fact that Mary is the Mother of God is a third reason why the Catholic Church honors her so highly.

I shall have more to say about Mary another time. Meanwhile, all that I have said brings to mind the story of Judith, a heroine of Jewish history. Do you remember her story as it is related in the Bible? A part of the Jewish people had been shut up in their city by a hostile army commanded by a general named Holofernes. Judith left the besieged city with her maid and was taken by the enemy. Because of her great beauty, she was invited to a banquet with Holofernes. Holofernes fell into a drunken stupor, and when all had withdrawn, Judith cut off his head with his own sword. Judith then made her way back to her own people. So heartened were the Jews by the death of Holofernes, so dismayed was the enemy, that the Jews broke the siege of their city. And, of course, Judith was honored by all.

Just as the Jews had been surrounded by a hostile army, so the sons and daughters of Adam were beset by sin. Just as Judith was instrumental in the destruction of her people's enemy, so Mary was instrumental in overcoming sin — by consenting to the incarnation and bearing her divine Son. Hence, the liturgy of the Catholic Church applies to Mary the praise which the Jews lavished upon Judith:

> "You are the glory of Jerusalem,
> the surpassing joy of Israel;
> you are the splendid boast of our people"
> (Jdt 15:9)

QUESTIONS FOR REVIEW

1. What do the Gospels tell us about Mary?
2. Why do Catholics and many other Christians esteem Mary so highly?
3. What is meant by the virginal conception of Jesus?
4. Was Mary the mother of children other than Jesus?
5. How are Judith and Mary similar?

CHAPTER 11

The Blessed Virgin Mary (II) HER PRIVILEGES

The first privilege conferred upon Mary in virtue of the fact that she is the Mother of God was her immaculate conception. To understand what this means, we must look back even beyond the immaculate conception itself. At the beginning of human history the parents of the human race rebelled against their Maker. They wished to become like gods. The result was that Adam and Eve and their descendants were estranged from their God and Father. Each child born into the world is the victim of this estrangement. Each child is infected with the sin of its first parents. This sinful infection in each one of us is called original sin because it comes down to us through our origin or descent from Adam. But Mary was an exception to the general rule. At no point in her life was she estranged from God. By a singular privilege she was preserved from the stain of original sin in the first instant of her conception. She was, as Catholics say, immaculately conceived.

Why do Catholics believe in Mary's immaculate conception? One reason is that they think of Christ as the "new Adam" and of Mary as the "new Eve," an idea that is sustained by the first chapter of Luke's Gospel. Just as Adam and Eve, the first parents of the human race, were created without sin so Jesus and Mary, the first members of a new race of graced individuals, appeared without sin.

In 1941, the Jewish novelist and playwright, Franz Werfel, wrote a book — later made into a movie — called *The Song of Bernadette*. The book and the movie were based on an event that occurred in 1858. The Blessed Virgin Mary appeared to a young French girl named Bernadette near the small town of Lourdes in southern France, and urged her to pray the rosary, pray for sinners, and do penance. A stream appeared in which the sick bathed and sometimes got better in a wonderful way. When Bernadette asked Mary's name, Mary referred to herself as the "Immaculate Conception." Subsequently, a great shrine was built at Lourdes to commemorate the event. Every year millions of pilgrims visit the shrine.

The story is told that during the filming of *The Song of Bernadette*, the Jewish producer used to ask Catholics whether they knew the difference between the virginal conception and the immaculate conception. By the virginal conception Catholics mean that Mary conceived Jesus without the intervention of a man through the overshadowing of the Holy Spirit. By the immaculate conception Catholics means that Mary was preserved from all stain of original sin.

But Catholic belief goes one step further. It holds that Mary, by a special privilege of God, was preserved not only from original sin, but also from actual sin; that is to say, she herself never contravened even the least commandment of God. Reflection upon Mary's divine maternity has strengthened the conviction of Catholics that Mary's holiness was flawless and immense.

Mary's absolute sinlessness throughout her life is explained by her closeness to Christ. The point is illustrated by Correggio's beautiful painting called "Holy Night." In the painting, Mary is bending over the Child who, however, does not appear in it. Over Mary's shoulder, Joseph can be seen standing in the shadow. The Virgin's face and body are alight with a brilliant soft splendor, as though she had embraced the sun. It is this proximity to the Son of God which explains Mary's fullness of grace and perfect sinlessness from the moment of her conception throughout her life. Jesus was the fountainhead, and Mary stood closest to this source of living water.

Catholic beleief maintains that at the end of her life Mary was taken or assumed, soul and body, into heaven. When ordinary mortals die, their bodies are placed in the ground to await the general resurrection at the end of the world. Mary's body was not allowed to corrupt. It was taken to heaven where it already shares the glory of the soul. In heaven Mary has been exalted above all creatures, and she reigns as queen of the universe.

Some years ago I had a discussion with two young Catholic ladies who were students at a public university. They said that they often discussed religion with other students. From time to time their friends asked them where Catholics find Mary's assumption in the Bible. Implied in this question is the supposition that all that Christians should believe is to be found in the Bible. This idea is not entirely correct.

We must remember that the apostles of Jesus began to teach his message on Pentecost, after the Holy Spirit had descended upon them. What the apostles taught was reflected in the life of the primitive Christian community — in its belief, its worship, and rules of conduct. When we Catholics speak of tradition, we are thinking of the life of the Christian community as an authentic reflection of the teaching of Christ and the apostles. Only later was the apostolic preaching written down in the books of the New Testament. And it took centuries to gather these books into the one volume that we know today. Hence, Catholics look not only to the Bible, but also to the belief and practices of the Church to discover authentic Christian doctrine. We Catholics believe that the Holy Spirit abides with the Church to preserve it in truth.

Having said this, I recall that Pope Pius XII, who solemnly taught the dogma of Mary's assumption in 1950, appealed to the Scriptures to support his teaching.[1] He noted several times the parallel between Adam and Eve on the one hand and Christ and Mary on the other — an idea sustained by the Gospels and found in the writings of the Fathers of the Church. Just as Eve shared the fate of Adam, so Mary shared the fate of her divine Son up to and including his resurrection from the dead. Just as Christ, the sinless One, triumphed over death, the consequence of sin, in his resurrection, so Mary, the sinless Mother of God, triumphed over death in her assumption. In any event, the belief of the Church, the pillar and ground of the truth (1 Tm 3:15), is sufficient to establish the fact of the assumption.

Mary is not only the mother of Jesus, but she is also our mother. In a very real sense Mary is the spiritual mother of the human race because, in subordination to her divine Son, she restored divine life to the human race. She did so by cooperating with her divine Son in the redemption of the human race — by consenting to his incarnation, giving him birth, caring for him, and sharing his sufferings on Calvary. The Second Vatican Council spoke of Mary as the mother of men and women in the order of grace.[2] In this context grace means divine life.

If Mary is our spiritual mother, then we ought to be devoted to her. Sons and daughters know instinctively how they should conduct themselves with respect to their earthly mothers. Catholics know instinctively how they should act with respect to their heavenly mother. By reason of her close association with her divine Son, we honor her with a special cult. We call her blessed because he who is mighty has done great things for her. We take refuge under her protection in our dangers and necessities. We invoke her intercession. We

1 *Munificentissimus Deus*, Nov. 1, 1950.
2 Constitution on the Church, nos. 61-62.

understand that true devotion to Mary means a recognition of her excellence, a filial love, and imitation of her virtues. We affirm that the honor shown to Mary redounds to the honor of her Son, for Mary's greatness lies in her relationship to her Son.

The favorite prayer of Catholics addressed to Mary, the Mother of God, is the "Hail Mary." Probably non-Catholics will not be very familiar with it. The "Hail Mary" was inspired largely by the Gospel of Luke. One recites the "Hail Mary" in this way: "Hail, Mary, full of grace; the Lord is with thee. Blessed art thou among women, and blessed is the fruit of thy womb, Jesus. Holy Mary, Mother of God, pray for us sinners now and at the hour of our death. Amen."

Catholics often pray the "Hail Mary" as part of the rosary. The rosary is a chain of fifty beads. As one fingers each bead, he or she recites the "Hail Mary." Each decade of ten beads is preceded by the recitation of the "Our Father" and concluded by a short prayer in honor of the Blessed Trinity. Usually a Catholic receives a rosary as a child; and one often sees it in the hands of a Catholic lying in the coffin.

QUESTIONS FOR REVIEW

1. What is meant by Mary's immaculate conception?
2. What is meant by the virginal conception of Jesus?
3. Was Mary free from actual sin?
4. Why do Catholics believe that Mary was assumed into heaven?
5. In what sense is Mary our mother?
6. How do Catholics express their devotion to Mary?
7. What is the rosary?

CHAPTER 12

GRACE

Today I wish to speak to you about grace, which is the fruit of Christ's death and resurrection.

What do Catholics means by the word, grace? Catholics understand grace to be a supernatural gift of God bestowed on us through the merits of Jesus Christ for our salvation. If a gift, such as the capacity to prophesy or heal, is bestowed upon a person for the benefit of others, then that gift is a kind of grace called a charism. For example, many a saint has been able to heal the sick in a wonderful way.

If, however, a gift is bestowed upon a person primarily for his or her own sanctification, then it is said to be a grace in the usual sense of the term. There are three kinds of grace given to individuals primarily for their own sanctification and salvation. They are uncreated grace and two kinds of created grace, namely, sanctifying grace and actual grace. I wish to say a word about each of these three kinds of grace.

Uncreated grace refers to the abiding presence of the Holy Trinity in the souls of God's friends. Perhaps you remember the words of Jesus in John's Gospel: "Whoever loves me will keep my word, and my Father will love him, and we will come to him and make our dwelling with him" (Jn 14:23). Furthermore, Jesus spoke of sending the Holy Spirit, the Advocate: "If I do not go [back to my Father], the Advocate will not come to you. But if I go, I will send him to you" (Jn 16:7). In other words, Jesus promised the indwelling of the triune God to the believer who receives Christ's commands and keeps them.

Then there is created or sanctifying grace. Uncreated grace and sanctifying grace are inseparable. Sanctifying grace is a created sharing in the life of God himself. Catholics find a reference or an allusion to sanctifying grace in the Bible wherever it speaks of being born again, of new life in the Spirit, or living on a higher plane of existence after repentance and belief. For example, in his conversation with Nicodemus in John's Gospel, Jesus said, "No one can enter the kingdom of God without being born of water and Spirit" (Jn 3:5). The new life that is given as a consequence of being born again of water and the Spirit Catholics call sanctifying grace. The difference between a person with sanctifying grace and a person without it is the difference between life and death. Those who are spiritually alive with sanctifying grace are adopted sons and daughters of God, they are temples of the Holy Trinity, and heaven is their inheritance.

Along with sanctifying grace come the supernatural virtues and the gifts of the Holy Spirit. The supernatural virtues include the theological virtues of faith, hope, and charity (1 Cor 13:13), and the moral virtues of which prudence, justice, fortitude, and temperance are the chief (Ws 8:7). The seven gifts of the Holy Spirit are wisdom, understanding, counsel, fortitude, knowledge, piety, and fear of the Lord (Is 11:2-3). The virtues help us to follow the guidance of reason and faith when we act, while the gifts help us to follow readily the inspirations of the Holy Spirit.

I have just spoken of being born again in connection with sanctifying grace. On this matter there is a measure of agreement and disagreement between Catholics and some Protestants. Both Catholics and Protestants agree that an individual must be born again after physical birth, that he or she must be raised to a new level of existence in order to enter the kingdom of God. Both Catholics and Protestants agree that an adult can be born again by committing oneself to God through Jesus Christ, if such commitment means repenting of one's sins, loving God above all things, and trusting in the sufficiency of Christ's death on Calvary. Catholics would add that even in this case an adult must be baptized if he or she is aware of the obligation (Mt 28:19).

However, there is a disagreement about the status of infants and children who do not have the use of reason. Catholics hold that these too must be born again since they have not been exempted from the fallen condition of humanity in general. Further, Catholics hold that such children are born again through the sacrament of baptism. In various places, the New Testament speaks of baptism as a new birth (Jn 3:5), a regeneration (Ti 3:5), a clothing with Christ (Gal 3:27). The new life which an infant receives through the sacrament of baptism Catholics call sanctifying grace. Indeed, the reception of sanctifying grace is the remission of original sin, for original sin is essentially the deprivation of sanctifying grace in newborns as the result of Adam's sin.

Catholics have always recognized the possibility of losing the friendship of God and sanctifying grace through serious sin — what Catholics call mortal sin. Just as one's physical life can be overtaken by death, so the life of the soul, sanctifying grace, can be overtaken by spiritual death through serious sin. The Bible tells us how some great friends of God, such as Moses, David, Solomon, and Peter fell into serious sin. Those sins are serious which the Bible or the Church describes as such, or which common sense recognizes as totally opposed to the love of God and neighbor. As examples of serious sins, I might mention hatred of God, murder, grave theft, adultery, and oppression of the poor. However, the sinner can recover the life of grace and the friendship of God by repenting of his sin and confessing it.

Catholics recognize the possibility of advancing in the

state of sanctifying grace. This takes place when God's life takes deeper root in the soul, when one's commitment to God and neighbor becomes stronger, when sin becomes less attractive. This is accomplished by keeping the commandments of God and fulfilling the demands of love.

Can we be absolutely certain that we have the grace of God and enjoy his friendship? We cannot doubt the mercy of God and the sufficiency of Christ's death on the cross. At the same time, we are aware of the hardness of our hearts and our inclination to sin, and so we cannot be absolutely certain that we have the grace of God. Nevertheless, there are certain signs which afford a measure of probability about the presence of grace in the soul. These signs include a delight in the things of God, contempt for what is sinful in the world, and the testimony of a good conscience which is unaware of any unrepented sin.

Then there is the matter of merit. Sanctifying grace renders the good works of the friend of God meritorious. The New Testament speaks of the reward which these works merit. For example, in his Letter to the Romans (2:5-7), Paul writes about "the just judgment of God, who will repay everyone according to his works: eternal life to those who seek glory, honor, and immortality through perseverance in good works." And in the First Letter of Peter (1:27), we read that God judges each one impartially on the basis of his works. Hence, one who is a friend of God through sanctifying grace can merit eternal life. However, far be it from the Christian to trust or glory in himself and not in the Lord (1 Cor 1:31). Merit is based on the free gift of God which is grace, so that God, the just judge, rewards and crowns his own gift. The relationship between grace and works has always been the subject of a lively debate between Catholics and Protestants, and I have been able to treat it only in summary fashion.

Finally, there is the reality of actual grace. This too along with sanctifying grace is a created reality. Actual grace is a transient help of God enlightening the mind and strengthening the will to do good and avoid evil. Catholics find a reference to actual grace in certain passages of the New Testament. In the Gospel of John, for example, Jesus says: "I am the vine, you are the branches. Whoever remains in me and I in him will bear much fruit, because without me you can do nothing" (Jn 15:5). "Without me you can do nothing" are the relevant words. And Paul writes: "God is the one who, for his good purpose, works in you both to desire and to work" (Ph 2:13). In these and other passages of the New Testament, Catholics find a reference to actual grace.

Perhaps we might compare actual grace to the current that starts an electric motor and keeps it running. Without the electric current the motor would not function. So too actual grace energizes the soul to do good and avoid evil.

We see, therefore, that one who has been born again truly lives on a new level of existence. The Holy Trinity dwells in the regenerated person as in a temple (uncreated grace); he or she is divinized by the presence of God's life in the soul (sanctifying grace); and there is a supernatural energy at work in God's son or daughter (actual grace).

QUESTIONS FOR REVIEW

1. What is grace?
2. What is meant by the divine indwelling?
3. What is sanctifying grace?
4. What are the supernatural virtues? The gifts of the Holy Spirit?
5. Can sanctifying grace be lost? Increased?
6. Can we be certain that we have sanctifying grace?
7. Do our good works merit a reward?
8. What is actual grace?

CHAPTER 13

SALVATION BY GRACE

Sometimes I am asked, "Do Catholics believe that we are saved by grace? How do Catholics understand the words of Paul: 'By grace you have been saved through faith, and this not from you; it is the gift of God; it is not from works, so no one may boast' (Ep 2:8-9)."

Surely Catholics believe that we are saved by grace. This is the teaching of Paul, which is part of the Bible, the word of God. What do Catholics mean when they say with Paul that by grace we have been saved through faith? They mean that salvation or the forgiveness of sins which is accompanied by the infusion of sanctifying grace is a gift of God bestowed on the sinner through faith which is acceptance of Jesus Christ and the gospel he proclaimed. Allow me to explain.

We may think of salvation in three ways.

We may think of it, first of all, as something achieved in the past. Salvation is the forgiveness of sins and new life effected by the death and resurrection of Jesus. At the Last Supper, for example, Jesus said that his blood would be shed for the forgiveness of sins (Mt 26:27-28). Indeed, he was given the name Jesus, which means "One who saves," because he was to save his people from their sins (Lk 2:21; Mt 1:21). The death and resurrection of Jesus were the means freely chosen by God to reconcile sinners to himself. Jesus thus made it possible for men and women to be forgiven and live anew. Of course, sinners must unite themselves to the death and resurrection of Jesus through faith and baptism in order to be saved. However, in one sense, salvation was achieved long ago when Jesus died and rose from the dead.

Secondly, we may think of salvation as the forgiveness of sins achieved in the present by the sinner who reforms his life and believes in the gospel. In this case, the forgiveness of sins and the life of grace are a gift of God, something completely unmerited. It is in this sense that we are to understand the quotation from Paul in the first paragraph.

However, we may not think that salvation can be finally and completely achieved in this life by a single act of faith. Remember Paul's words: "Whoever thinks he is standing secure should take care not to fall" (1 Cor 10:12). And elsewhere Paul wrote: "I drive my body and train it, for fear that, after having preached to others, I myself should be disqualified" (1 Cor 9:27). The New Testament teaches very clearly that the salvation conferred by the death of Christ and received by faith is real and genuine, but is capable of growth and subject to loss.

Thirdly, we may think of salvation as a reality finally and completely achieved, no longer capable of growth or subject to loss. In this sense, salvation is a future reality that we shall possess at the end of our lives when we are admitted to the eternal life of heaven. Salvation, understood in this sense, does depend upon our good works. This idea is impressed upon Catholics by the scene in Matthew's Gospel where all nations are assembled before the glorified Savior. In that scene those who have practiced the works of mercy are rewarded with eternal life, while those who have not are excluded from it (Mt 25:31-46). Then, there are the words of Paul. Looking back over his life, Paul wrote to Timothy: "My departure is at hand. I have competed well; I have finished the race; I have kept the faith. From now on the crown of righteousness awaits me, which the Lord, the just judge, will award to me on that day" (2 Tm 4:6-8).

So we understand from these passages and many others in the New Testament that our eternal salvation does depend upon our good works. However, even in this case it is God who has established the reward and brings to fruition the unmerited forgiveness of the sinner.

Sometimes Catholics are asked by non-Catholics: "Have you been saved?" Catholics may reply: "Yes, I have been saved by the death and resurrection of Jesus and by my commitment to him. But I still have to work hard to gain my eternal salvation in heaven."

QUESTIONS FOR REVIEW

1. What is the meaning of grace in its most general sense?
2. What is salvation?
3. Is salvation a gift?
4. Have you been saved?

CHAPTER 14

The Church (I)
ITS FOUNDATION

Today I should like to speak about the Church, especially, the Catholic Church, which is, in a sense, the extension of Christ in space and time.

Sometimes we use the word, church, to designate the building in which Christians meet; but it refers primarily to the people who meet in that building, that is to say, to Christians, the followers of Jesus Christ. Jesus himself is the founder of the Church. Just as Jewish rabbis gathered disciples around themselves in order to instruct them in the Law, so Jesus gathered followers or disciples around himself in order to instruct them in the things of God. From the circle of his disciples, Jesus selected twelve of them that they might be with him and he might send them forth to preach (Mk 3:14). By gathering disciples, by choosing the Twelve, by entrusting them with the mission of preaching to others, Jesus established in effect a religious society. By so doing, he took an important first step in the establishment of the Church which is a group of persons committed to Jesus and to the proclamation of his message.

Jesus took a second step in the establishment of his Church when he chose the apostle Peter to be the foundation of his Church. At Caesarea Philippi, Jesus said to Peter, "You are Peter [which means rock], and upon this rock I will build my church, and the gates of the netherworld shall not prevail against it" (Mt 16:18). In the same place Jesus promised Peter the keys of the kingdom of heaven and the authority to bind and loose (Mt 16:19). Then, after his resurrection, Jesus explicitly made Peter the shepherd of his flock. After Peter had declared his love for Jesus, Jesus said to Peter: "Feed my lambs . . . tend my sheep" (Jn 21:15-16). In this way Jesus provided his Church with visible leadership, once he had withdrawn from this earth.

Jesus took a third step in the establishment of his Church when he forged a new covenant and a new people of God who constitute the Church. Jesus did so at the Last Supper which he observed in anticipation of his death on the cross. "While they were eating, he took bread, said the blessing, broke it, and gave it to them, and said, 'Take it; this is my body.' Then he took a cup, gave thanks, and gave it to them, and they all drank from it. He said to them, 'This is my blood of the covenant, which will be shed for many' " (Mk 14:22-24). In this way, Jesus made a new covenant between God and his earthly sons and daughters and established the Church as the new people of God.

Jesus took a fourth step in the establishment of his Church: he sent his representatives to every nation and generation. Jesus said to his disciples: "All power in heaven and on earth has been given to me. Go, therefore, and make disciples of all nations, baptizing them in the name of the Father, and of the Son, and of the Holy Spirit, teaching them to observe all that I have commanded you. And behold, I am with you always, until the end of the age" (Mt 28:18-20).

Finally, on Pentecost Jesus sent the Holy Spirit upon his followers, the Church. He did so in accordance with his promise: "I will ask the Father, and he will give you another Advocate to be with you always" (Jn 14:16). In the Old Testament, in the Book of Joel, God had promised his spirit to those who lived under the new covenant (Jl 3:1). On Pentecost this promise was fulfilled (Ac 2:14-21).

By a series of steps, therefore, Jesus founded the Church. A review of these steps enables us to achieve some understanding of the nature of the Church. The Church is a community of persons committed to Jesus Christ and the spread of his message. This community is the new people of God. It possesses the Holy Spirit and the visible leadership of Peter and the apostles. On another occasion I shall explain why I believe that the Church founded by Jesus and the Catholic Church are one and the same.

The New Testament has a great deal to say about the Church founded by Jesus Christ. For example, the New Testament is deeply impregnated with the thought that the Christian community or Church has become the new Israel, the new people of God. In other words, the Christian community or Church has the same relationship to God under the New Testament which the Israelites claimed for themselves under the Old Testament. The thought that the Christian Church is the new Israel, the new people of God, was expressed by Paul with particular emphasis.

One of the most important images employed by the Apostle Paul to describe the Church is the body of Christ. In antiquity it was common to compare a community whose members shared a common life to a living organism. Paul compared the Church to a human body. Just as the members of a human body — the eye, the ear, the foot — have different functions which serve the whole body, so the members of the Church have different functions which serve the whole Church (1 Cor 12:12-31; Rm 12:4-5). However, Paul goes on to refine this idea: the Church is not just a body; it is the body of Christ; indeed, it is Christ. Paul wrote: "As a body is one though it has many parts, and all the parts of the body, though many, are one body, so also Christ" (1 Cor 12:12). In this latter case, Paul identifies Christ and the Church.

Paul used many other beautiful images to describe the Church Jesus founded. In one passage, Paul wrote to the Christians at Corinth: "I betrothed you to one husband to present you as a chaste virgin to Christ" (2 Cor 11:2). This remark means that Paul, by his missionary activity among the Corinthians, had brought them to Christ as a father presents his daughter to her husband.

For Paul, the Church is also a building or a temple. He wrote to the Corinthians: "You are God's field, God's building. . . . Like a wise master builder I laid a foundation, and another is building upon it. But each one must be careful how he builds upon it, for no one can lay a foundation other than the one that is there, namely, Jesus Christ. . . . Do you not know that you are the temple of God, and that the Spirit of God dwells in you?" (1 Cor 3:9-16).

The New Testament tells how the Holy Spirit builds up the Church in a variety of ways. The Spirit was responsible for certain extraordinary gifts enjoyed by the early Christians (1 Cor 12:4-11). The Spirit unites the members of the Church among themselves so that, many as they are, they form one body which is the Church (1 Cor 12:13). The Spirit provides for order in the Church where he placed bishops to rule the Church of God (Ac 20:28). The Holy Spirit remains with the apostles forever (Jn 14:16-17). He does so in order to teach and remind them of what Christ said (Jn 14:26).

The New Testament also describes the Christian Church as a sojourner in this world. This idea appears especially in the Pauline literature and the Gospel of John. As "saints" and "chosen ones" Christians have been taken out of the world and separated from "those outside." As a result, the early Christians experienced a feeling of alienation from the world. Hence, they were "strangers" and "sojourners" in this world (Heb 11:13; 1 P 2:11); and Christians were obliged to be "blameless and innocent, children of God without blemish in the midst of a crooked and perverse generation" (Ph 2:15). As the people of God upon earth, Christians have here no lasting city, but seek the one that is to come (Heb 13:14). Their citizenship is in heaven (Ph 3:20). Because the gospel is foolishness to those who are perishing (1 Cor 1:18), the world hates Christians and this hatred is proof that they do not belong to the world (Jn 15:18-21). Christians are in the world (Jn 17:11), but not of it (Jn 17:14-16). They live in the world with the certainty that it is passing away (1 Cor 7:31).

QUESTIONS FOR REVIEW

1. What is the meaning of the word, Church?
2. How did Jesus found the Church?
3. In what sense is the Church the new people of God?
4. What are some images of the Church in the New Testament?

CHAPTER 15

The Church (II)
ITS IDENTITY TODAY

On this occasion I should like to explain why I believe that the Church founded by Jesus Christ and the Catholic Church are one and the same. I wish to offer three reasons for this belief.

My first reason. Jesus founded his Church upon the apostle Peter. He said to Peter in the neighborhood of Caesarea Philippi: "You are Peter [which means rock], and upon this rock I will build my church" (Mt 16:18). In the same place Jesus promised Peter the keys of the kingdom of heaven and the authority to bind and loose (Mt 16:19). Then, after his resurrection, Jesus explicitly made Peter the shepherd of his flock. After Peter had declared his love for Jesus, Jesus said to him: "Feed my lambs . . . tend my sheep" (Jn 21:15-17). In this way, Jesus provided his Church with visible leadership, once he has withdrawn from this earth. Now, however, the Church is led by the successors of Peter, the Popes, the bishops of Rome where Peter died and handed down the mantle of leadership. Therefore, those followers of Christ — Catholics — who recognize the religious leadership of the Popes constitute the Church of Christ. Of course, Jesus himself remains the invisible head of the Church.

There is a second reason. It is the catholicity or universality of the Catholic Church. The word, catholic, means universal. Jesus himself spoke of the universality of his Church. He sent his representatives to preach the gospel to all nations until the end of time. He promised to stand by his representatives as they carried out the mission entrusted to them (Mt 28:19-20). Jesus foresaw the success of the mission and anticipated the universality of his Church. He said: "Many will come from the east and the west, and will recline with Abraham, Isaac, and Jacob at the banquet in the kingdom of heaven" (Mt 8:11). He also told his followers: "You will be my witnesses in Jerusalem, throughout Judea and Samaria, and to the ends of the earth" (Ac 1:8). The Church must be catholic or universal because it plays a vital role in implementing the universal mediatorship of Jesus. All of which is to say that the Church of Christ has a conspicuous number of members throughout the world.

The Catholic Church, however, is truly remarkable among all other Christian bodies for its catholicity or universality. One finds Catholics in the remotest places on this earth. I remember my experience in the African country of Tanzania. Our party was traveling on a lonely road to a game park. All we could see in any direction were vast stretches of dry grass, some thorn trees, and a few giraffes. Suddenly we saw a cloud of dust in the distance. A small truck was approaching us from the opposite direction. Finally it passed us; and as it did, I read the letters on the side of the truck: "Catholic Hospital of Tanzania." The Catholic Church was present even in that remote spot.

The Catholic Church is catholic or universal in the sense that it has a conspicuous number of members throughout the world. In fact, the number of Catholics greatly exceed the number of all other Christians taken together. Other Christian communities approach only remotely the universal diffusion of the Catholic Church. The Catholic Church embraces men and women of every continent, of every race and color, of every language and culture background, of every economic and social condition. The universality of the Catholic Church is uniquely consistent with the universality of the Church of Christ, as it is described in the New Testament. Hence, Catholics see in the catholicity or universality of their Church evidence that it is Christ's Church.

There is a third reason why I believe that Jesus Christ founded the Catholic Church. It is the stability of that Church. Allow me to quote the words of the nineteenth century English historian, Thomas Macaulay, about this. Macaulay, a non-Catholic, wrote: "There is not, and there never was on this earth, a work of human policy so well deserving of examination as the Roman Catholic Church. The history of that Church joins together the two great ages of human civilization. No other institution is left standing which carries the mind back to the time when the smoke of sacrifice rose from the Pantheon, and when camelopards and tigers bounded in the Flavian Amphitheatre."

Macaulay continued: "The proudest royal houses are but of yesterday when compared with the line of Supreme Pontiffs. That line we trace back in an unbroken series from the Pope who crowned Napoleon in the nineteenth century to the Pope who crowned Pepin in the eighth; and far beyond the time of Pepin the august dynasty extends, till it is lost in the twillight of fable. The Republic of Venice came next in antiquity; and the Republic of Venice is gone, and the Papacy remains. The Papacy remains, not in decay, not a mere antique, but full of life and youthful vigor. The Catholic Church is still sending forth to the farthest ends of the world missionaries as zealous as those who landed in Kent with Augustine, and still confronting hostile kings with the same spirit with which she confronted Attila. The number of her children is greater than in any former age. Her acquisitions in the New World have more than compensated her for what she lost in the Old. . . ."

Macaulay concluded his remarks about the stability of the Catholic Church by saying: "We see no sign which indicates that the term of her long dominion is approaching. She saw the commencement of all governments and of all ecclesiastical establishments that now exist in the world; and we feel no assurance that she is not destined to see the end of them all. She was great and respected before the Saxon had set foot on Britain, before the Frank had passed the Rhine, when Grecian eloquence still flourished in Antioch, when idols were still worshipped in the temple of Mecca. And she may still exist in undiminished vigor when some traveler from New Zealand shall, in the midst of a vast solitude, take his stand on a broken arch of London Bridge to sketch the ruin of St. Paul's."[1]

What is the significance of the stability of the Catholic Church so vividly described by Macaulay? The answer, I believe, is this: It is the fate of human societies with a very large membership to change, fragmentize, and disappear with the passage of time. Human history testifies to the appearance and dissolution of countless political institutions, religious sects, and social organizations. Yet the Catholic Church has not disappeared with the passage of the centuries. Indeed, it remains "not in decay, not a mere antique, but full of youthful vigor," as Macaulay wrote. One must conclude that the Catholic Church is not sustained by human resources, but by the extraordinary intervention of God on its behalf. The words of Gamaliel are to the point: "If this endeavor or this activity is of human origin, it will destroy itself. But if it comes from God, you will not be able to destroy them" (Ac 5:38-39).

The Catholic Church is itself a sign that it comes from God and Jesus Christ. As a divine work, it claims a divine mission and a divine message. If a Catholic is asked why he or she is a member of the Catholic Church, the Catholic ought to reply that he or she is a Catholic because Jesus Christ founded the Catholic Church.

1 T.B. Macaulay, *The Miscellaneous Works, Critical and Historical Essays*, New York, 4, 366-367.

QUESTIONS FOR REVIEW

1. How does the leadership of the Pope show that Jesus founded the Catholic Church?
2. How does the catholicity of the Catholic Church do so?
3. How does the stability of the Catholic Church do so?

CHAPTER 16

The Church (III)
ITS TEACHING AUTHORITY

Today I should like to address the question of the teaching authority or "magisterium" of the Church. By this, I mean the right and duty of the Church to teach the message of Christ.

The teaching authority of the Church rests upon the great commission given the Church by its departing Lord. At the conclusion of his earthly life Jesus said to his disciples: "All power in heaven and on earth has been given to me. Go, therefore, and make disciples of all nations, baptizing them in the name of the Father, and of the Son, and of the Holy Spirit, teaching them to observe all that I have commanded you. And behold I am with you always, until the end of the age" (Mt 28:18-20). Jesus told his disciples that they were to be witnesses to him "in Jerusalem, throughout Judea and Samaria, and to the ends of the earth" (Ac 1:8). Therefore, the Church has the right and duty to preach the gospel to every nation and generation in virtue of the mandate of Christ.

At the conclusion of his great commission to the Church to preach the gospel, Jesus told his disciples: "Behold, I am with you always, until the end of the age" (Mt 28:20). These words express the promise of Christ to stand by his representatives as they carry out the mandate to teach his message to others. He will help them to implement the task he has entrusted to them. This is the meaning of the infallibility which the Church claims for itself — that at any moment the Church teaches the message of Christ, and not something else, because of the promise of Christ.

In the judgment of Catholics, the Pope and the bishops exercise the teaching authority of the Church because they are the successors of Peter and the original apostles: they have inherited their burdens and responsibilities. What Peter and the original apostles were to the primitive Church, that the Pope and the bishops are to the contemporary Church.

The Pope exercises the infallible teaching authority of the Church when he defines a doctrine of faith or morals in his capacity as the visible head of the Church. In this case, the Pope is said to be speaking *ex cathedra.* A doctrine of faith or morals means a teaching having to do with beliefs or practice. The Pope cannot invent such a doctrine. It must be something that Christ taught or connected with his teaching. For example, in 1854 Pope Pius IX defined the doctrine of Mary's immaculate conception, and in 1950 Pope Pius XII defined the doctrine of Mary's assumption into heaven. Both of these doctrines suppose Mary's relationship to Christ and her redemption by him.

As a matter of fact, the Pope exercises his infallible teaching authority on relatively few occasions. However, he constantly teaches with a lesser degree of authority. For example, recent Popes have written and taught about such topics as the relationship between the Church and the secular State, the Bible, education, marriage, the rights of workers, public worship, the communications media, and economic justice on an international level. The Popes have written and taught about such topics in the light of Christian principles. The Popes did not intend to speak infallibly about these matters, but they did expect Catholics to accept their teaching inasmuch as they are divinely appointed teachers in the Church.

The bishops exercise the infallible teaching authority of the Church in two different situations — when they are gathered together in an ecumenical council and even when they are dispersed throughout the world in the areas entrusted to their supervision.

From time to time the bishops of the Catholic Church gather together in one place to discuss questions of universal concern. Such a gathering is called an ecumenical council. In the course of their deliberations the bishops may choose to define a doctrine of faith or morals, a matter of belief or practice. In this case, they teach infallibly in their capacity as the successors of the apostles and leaders of the Church. The most recent ecumenical council was the Second Vatican Council which gathered in Rome in the 1960's. However, the bishops of this council did not choose to define any doctrine.

The bishops also exercise the infallible teaching authority of the Church when they are dispersed throughout the world in the areas intrusted to their supervision. While the Pope is the chief shepherd of the universal Church, a bishop is the chief shepherd of a particular Church and geographical area. Accordingly, we have the bishop of Paris, the bishop of Berlin, the bishop of New York, and so on. As its shepherd, each bishop must teach the Church intrusted to him. When the bishops in these circumstances agree among themselves that a particular doctrine pertains to the message of Christ, they teach Christ's doctrine infallibly. It is my opinion that in this way the bishops have infallibly taught many of the truths of morality such as the sinfulness of adultery, stealing, and disobedience to lawful authority.

I must note, however, that each bishop as an individual does not enjoy the prerogative of infallibility, as the Pope does. A bishop can err in his teaching. Nevertheless, as a divinely appointed teacher in the Church, he can rightly expect the assent of his people to his teaching. If there is error, it will become apparent by contrast with the teaching of the universal Church.

The Second Vatican Council expressed confidence that the teaching of the Pope and bishops would always gain the assent of their people. Christ's Holy Spirit, who enlightens the teachers of the Church, also preserves the whole flock of Christ in the unity of faith. As a result, the body of the faithful as a whole cannot err in matters of belief. In this sense the whole Church is a repository of Christian truth.

Earlier I remarked that the object of the Church's teaching authority is something that Christ taught or something connected with his teaching. What Christ taught, what is connected with his teaching, is found in the Bible and in the belief and practice of the Church. This body of truth is sometimes called the deposit of revelation, that is to say, something made known by God especially through his Son Jesus Christ and preserved for us by the Church.

We see, therefore, that the teaching authority of the Church rests upon the great commission given the Church by Christ, the commission to teach all nations what he had taught. This teaching authority is vested in the Pope and bishops, the leaders of the Church, the successors of Peter and the apostles. He who hears them hears the voice of Christ.[1] It's just as simple as that.

1 My remarks on this occasion have been drawn, for the most part, from the Second Vatican Council's Constitution on the Church, no. 25.

QUESTIONS FOR REVIEW

1. What is the teaching authority or magisterium of the Church?

2. Why does the Church have the authority to teach?
3. What is the meaning of the Church's infallibility?
4. Who exercises the teaching authority of the Church? Why?
5. In what circumstances does the Pope teach infallibly?
6. In what circumstances do the bishops teach infallibly?
7. When do the Pope and bishops teach on a lower level of authority?
8. In what sense is the *whole* Church infallible?
9. What is the object of the Church's teaching authority?

CHAPTER 17

The Church (IV)
THE LAITY

At this point I should like to say a word about the lay members of the Church. My remarks are drawn largely from the statements of the Second Vatican Council (1962-65).[1]

By the laity or lay members of the Church I mean the great body of Catholics who are neither clergy nor members of a religious congregation. The lay members of the Church are part of the people of God, the Church of Christ. Lay people have been dedicated to the mission of the Church by their reception of baptism and confirmation. They seek the kingdom of God by their involvement in material and secular affairs. They are absorbed by family, social, and business concerns. They participate in the trades and professions. In this way they carry out the plan of God for the world. They make the Church present and active in those situations accessible to them alone.

The laity share in the priesthood of Christ by lives of sacrifice and especially by their participation in the Holy Eucharist. They share in the prophetic office of Christ by giving witness to him and living the gospel in the world. They share in the kingly office of Christ by bringing all things,

1 Constitution on the Church, especially cc. 4-5, and the Decree of the Apostolate of the Laity.

including themselves, into subjection to the Father. The laity are encouraged to recognize the meaning and value of created things. By their technical skills and cultural endowments they can assist all human beings to benefit from created goods. By striving for a just social order they can prepare the field of the world for the seed of the gospel.

The providence of God assigns to each member of the laity the area in which he or she is to act. The role of husbands and wives is of unique importance for the fulfillment of the mission of the Church. They are the first to communicate to their children the good news of the kingdom of God. They care for each other as both seek the kingdom together. They defend the dignity and autonomy of the family in accordance with Christian principles. Moreover, the family can further the mission of the Church by such activities as these: the adoption of abandoned infants, hospitality to strangers, advice and material assistance to adolescents, help to engaged couples as they prepare for marriage, catechetical work, the support of married couples involved in material and moral crises, and assistance to the aged, not only by providing them with the necessities of life, but also by obtaining for them a fair share of the benefits of an expanding economy.

The role of citizens — an indispensable one for the mission of the Church — is to infuse a Christian spirit into the mentality, customs, laws, and structures of the community in which they live. A variety of means is available to them for this purpose. By expressing their opinion, through the ballot let us say, citizens can influence civil authorities to act with justice toward all. As public officials, citizens can uphold the laws of the community and serve the common good. Indeed, in a public or private capacity, they can cooperate in many praiseworthy projects. Citizens are in a position to research into civil and social practices. They have the opportunity to foster the spirit of brotherhood. They serve a useful function when they form international associations, which are especially desirable at this time when contacts between nations are becoming more numerous and complicated. In other words, any contribution which citizens make to the development of material, technical, and cultural resources serves the mission of the Church.

While the activity of the laity which I have just described supposes to some extent a particular set of circumstances, every individual, no matter what his or her situation may be, can cooperate in the fulfillment of the Church's mission. The testimony of a good life serves this end. Every lay man and woman can speak to others about the Church. Moreover, he or she can reach others in an important way by prayer, penance, public and private worship, and good works.

The laity, beyond pursuing the renewal of the temporal order, also have the opportunity to assist the clergy more directly in their work of evangelizing and sanctifying. Instances of such direct cooperation would be these: active participation in the public worship of the Church as readers and distributors of Holy Communion, teaching sacred doctrine to the uninstructed, serving in institutions sponsored by the Church, editing publications concerned with the Church's mission, promoting the interests of the Church in the public forum, and other activities of a similar nature.

To be sure, the order of the Church requires that the laity be united with those whom the Lord has chosen to lead his Church. At the same time, the laity should reveal their needs and desires to the pastors of the Church. By reason of their knowledge and ability, they are permitted and sometimes even obliged to express their opinion on those matters which concern the good of the Church.

Effective cooperation in the mission of the Church supposes on the part of the laity a certain degree of natural ability and a capacity for good human relations. These resources must be augmented by a suitable knowledge of Catholic doctrine. Finally, and very importantly, the laity should undertake to preserve their union with Christ, meditate on the word of God, aspire to spiritual riches, maintain a certain indifference to temporal goods, and dedicate themselves to the advancement of the kingdom of God.

There are many helps for persons who wish to cooperate more effectively in the mission of the Church, such things as study sessions, congresses, periods of retreat, spiritual exercises, periodicals, books, and the new methods of communication and social action.

All the members of the Church including the laity are called to be holy. On another occasion I spoke about sanctifying grace. I said that sanctifying grace was equivalent to a new life, the result of being born again in baptism or by repentance and belief. Holy men and women rejoice in the new life of sanctifying grace. In the language of the New Testament, they are adopted sons and daughters of God; they are sharers in the divine nature; they are disciples and followers of Christ; they keep his commandments and carry their cross after him; they love God above all things and love others because of God.

On another occasion too I said that holiness can be intensified, that the new life of sanctifying grace is capable of increased vigor. Holiness is intensified when Christians live as a holy people, when they strive for greater conformity to the will of God. The will of God makes different demands upon different individuals. The ministers of the Church, for example, are expected to serve their people. This service should be the principal means of their growth in holiness. Married couples grow in holiness by generous love for one another and their children. Widows, widowers, and single persons grow in holiness by fulfilling their responsibilities. Laborers can conform themselves to Christ who was a carpenter. Those who suffer poverty, sickness, and persecution can unite themselves with the suffering Christ who called them blessed. Christians can grow in holiness in and through the conditions, duties, and circumstances of their lives, if they accept everything from the hand of God.

Holiness means loving God above all things and loving others because of God. Holiness and love are nurtured by listening to the word of God, by the reception of the sacraments, by prayer, self-denial, fraternal charity, and the practice of the virtues and evangelical counsels. The latter were recommended by Jesus to his disciples. They are poverty, chastity, and obedience.

QUESTIONS FOR REVIEW

1. Who are the laity?
2. What is their proper field of activity?
3. How do lay persons share in the priestly, prophetic, and kingly offices of Christ?
4. How do husbands and wives further the mission of the Church?
5. How do citizens further the mission of the Church?
6. What can every lay person do to further the mission of the Church?
7. How can the laity assist the ordained ministers of the Church?
8. What can the laity do to become more effective members of the Church?
9. How do the laity grow in holiness?

CHAPTER 18

The Bible (I)
ITS MAKEUP

Today I wish to speak to you about the Bible. The Bible is the book of the Church. This is so for two reasons: it enshrines the belief of the Church, and it has been given into the care of the Church for preservation and interpretation. I hasten to add, however, that even though the Bible is the book of the Church, the Church stands under the judgment of the Bible.

The Bible consists of the Old and New Testaments. The Old Testament books were written before the birth of Christ, and the New Testament books were written after the birth of Christ.

The composition of the Old Testament was a process that took over a thousand years. Some portions of the Old Testament, like the Song of Miriam in the Book of Exodus (15:1-21) and the Song of Deborah in the Book of Judges (5), probably go back to the twelfth century B.C. The latest books in the Old Testament of the Catholic Bible, Second Maccabees and Wisdom, were composed about 100 B.C. During this long period of composition there was a gradual accumulation of material into books and then into collections of books.

In the Old Testament we can distinguish, first of all, the Pentateuch, which consists of the first five books of the Bible, namely, Genesis, Exodus, Leviticus, Numbers, and Deuteronomy. The Pentateuch enjoys particular prestige among religious Jews as the "Law" or "Torah," which is the concrete expression of God's will for them. But the Pentateuch is more than a body of legal doctrine, for it tells the story of the formation of the people of God: the story of Abraham and the patriarchs, of Moses and the Hebrew people.

Then there are the historical books of the Old Testament. These include Joshua, Judges, First and Second Samuel, First and Second Kings, First and Second Chronicles, Ezra, Nehemiah, and First and Second Maccabees. To these are added the special literary group of Tobit, Judith, and Esther. These books tell the history of the Israelites from the death of Moses to the days of Samuel, Saul, and David to the days of the Maccabees and the attempt to suppress Judaism in the second century B.C.

Besides the Pentateuch and the historical books, we can identify another group of books in the Old Testament. That group comprises the Wisdom books. These include the Books of Job, Psalms, Proverbs, Ecclesiastes, the Song of Songs, Wisdom, and Sirach. The chief purpose of these books is instruction. The wisdom of the Bible is the fruit of a movement among ancient oriental peoples to gather, preserve, and express the results of human experience as an aid to understanding and solving the problems of life.

Finally, there are the prophetic books. These include, for example, the relatively long books of Isaiah, Jeremiah, and Ezekiel, and the shorter books of Joel, Amos, and Micah. The prophets were the spokesmen of God, intermediaries between him and his people. The prophetic books of the Bible reflect the preaching of the prophets. Some parts of the prophetic books were written by the prophets themselves, some by persons other than the prophets. The prophets judged the moral conduct of the people on the basis of the alliance between God and Israel. The prophets taught sublime truths and lofty morals. They exhorted, threatened, announced punishment, and promised deliverance. The prophets were concerned primarily with the interests of God, especially in reference to Israel. They denounced idolatry and worship that was not internalized. They were also concerned with the universal nature of the moral law, personal responsibility, the person and office of the Messiah, and the conduct of foreign nations.

As I remarked at the beginning, the composition of the Old Testament was a process that took over a thousand years. The Jews recognized the books of the Old Testament as sacred and used them in their worship. When the Christian Church was in its formative period after the ascension of Christ, it continued to use the sacred books of the Jews for worship and inspiration. And that's how the books of the Old Testament became part of the Christian Bible.

Up to this point, I have been speaking about the Old Testament. Now I wish to say a word about the New Testament which is the second part of the Christian Bible.

The early followers of Jesus had, as I said, the Old Testament. As long as the apostles and the immediate disciples of Jesus were still alive, there was no pressing need for Christian writings. In fact, we have no clear proof of major Christian writings from the period immediately after Jesus' ascension (A.D. 30-50). During this time the Christian faith was communicated by preaching and by the life and practices of the Christian community — by what Catholics call tradition. But then the situation changed. Two things were at work:

The first thing was the missionary activity of the early Church. Missionaries founded Christian communities the length and breadth of the known world. As the missionaries continued to travel, they had to communicate with their converts by writing. Instruction had to come from afar. This need was first met by letters and epistles, and the letters of Paul are the earliest major Christian writings of which we know with certainty. Most of these were written as instruction and encouragement to Churches that Paul himself had evangelized. First and Second Thessalonians were written in the early 50's; and the so-called Great Letters, namely, Galatians, First and Second Corinthians, Romans, and perhaps Philippians, were written in the late 50's. The Captivity Letters, so-called because they were written while Paul was in prison, appeared in the early 60's. These are Philemon, Colossians, and Ephesians. Traditionally, the Pastoral Letters of First and Second Timothy and Titus have been dated in the mid-60's. In all, there were thirteen letters or epistles.

The second thing was the need to preserve the memory of Jesus' words and deeds. The desire to meet this need ultimately gave rise to the Gospels. The Gospels, too, are a part of the New Testament. Probably, the Gospel of Mark was written in the 60's. That of Matthew was written in the 70's or more likely in the 80's. Luke most likely wrote his Gospel and his history of the early Church, the Acts of the Apostles, in the 80's. Then, in the 90's a disciple of John, the son of Zebedee, produced a Gospel somewhat different than the others.

There are still other writings in the New Testament. There is the Book of Revelation or Apocalypse, the last book of the Christian Bible. It is a strange book because it abounds in unfamiliar and extravagant symbolism. There is the Epistle to the Hebrews which was probably written by a Jewish Christian well educated in the literary style of the Greek language. Then there are the seven so-called Catholic Epistles. These are the letters of James; First, Second and Third John; First and Second Peter; and Jude. They are called Catholic Epistles because, in general, they were directed to the whole Church and not to a specific group.

We are very poorly informed about the composition and collection of these letters. In any event, however, by the end of the fourth century in the Latin and Greek Churches there was general acceptance of these twenty-seven books of the New Testament, the ones Catholics recognize today. These books were being read in the public worship of the Christian Church along with the books of the Old Testament.

It is apparent from the history of the formation of the Christian Bible that it took many years, even centuries, before the universal Church was aware of, and able to collect, all the Gospels and letters of the New Testament from the widely scattered Churches to whom they were addressed. No matter! The teaching of Christ was being proclaimed by the preachers and preserved in the institutions and practices of the Church.

QUESTIONS FOR REVIEW

1. Why is the Bible the book of the Church?
2. How do we divide the books of the Old Testament?
3. Why did Christians write the books of the New Testament?
4. How do we divide the books of the New Testament?
5. When were the books of the New Testament finally gathered together?

CHAPTER 19

The Bible (II)
THE WORD OF GOD

Why did Catholics admit only the forty-five books of the Old Testament and the twenty-seven books of the New Testament into their Bible? We know that both the ancient Jews and the early Christians composed other religious books which were never admitted into the Catholic Bible. For example, Christians composed other gospels known as the Gospel of Thomas, the Gospel of Peter, and the Gospel of James. Why then did the Church accept only the four Gospels of Matthew, Mark, Luke, and John into the Bible and exclude the others? The reason is that the present collection of Biblical books, including the four Gospels, and that collection alone, was considered to have been written under the inspiration of the Holy Spirit. God was the author of the books included in the Bible.

The belief in the divine origin of the books of the Old Testament is common to Jews and Christians. The Jews of Jesus' day firmly believed that God had communicated the text of the Old Testament to the inspired writers. The New Testament quotes the Old Testament about three hundred and fifty times in such a way as to show that Jesus and the writers of the New Testament shared the belief of Judaism in the divine origin and authority of the books of the Old Testament. Speaking of the Old Testament, Paul wrote to Timothy: "All scripture is inspired by God and is useful for teaching, for refutation, for correction, and for training in righteousness, so that the one who belongs to God may be competent, equipped for every good work" (2 Tm 3:16-17).

The Christian belief in the divine origin of the New Testament came about only gradually. When Christians composed their own religious writings, they considered some of them as sacred and read them in the course of divine worship. They came to regard these writings as equal in authority to the books of the Old Testament. The sacred books of the Christians had been written by apostolic men and expressed the faith of the apostolic Church. However, the same Spirit, who had inspired the prophets of old, had descended upon these apostolic men who were the successors of the prophets. Moreover, the same Spirit, who had preserved and nurtured the faith of the Church, had been active in the composition of the sacred books which reflected the faith of the Church. Christians concluded, therefore, that God was also the author of the books which we now know as the New Testament.

From this account we understand what a decisive role the Church played in the collection of the Biblical books. It was the Church which identified the inspired books of the Bible and brought them together in one volume. As St. Augustine (354-430), perhaps the greatest of the Fathers of the Church, wrote: "I would not believe the gospel did not the authority of the Catholic Church move me to this."[1]

What do Catholics mean when they say that God is the author of the Bible? Pope Leo XIII answered that question in 1893. In a document beginning with the Latin words, *Providentissimus Deus*, Pope Leo wrote: "God so moved the inspired writers by his supernatural operation that he incited them to write and assisted them in their writings, so that they carefully conceived, accurately wrote down, and truthfully

1 *Contra epist, Manich.*, 5, 6.

expressed all that he intended and only what he intended; and only in this way can God be the author of the Bible."

Although God is the author of Sacred Scripture, it is also true that human beings made their own contribution to the production of the sacred books. The human writers employed their faculties and powers in the composition of the Bible. God assumed the entire man as a concrete reality with his date and situation in history, his personality, and his habits of thought and speech. God applied all these things to writing the book that God intended, but the individuals whom God employed left their mark upon their writing. And so, for example, we have the fine Greek style of the Letter to the Hebrews and the less felicitous style of some other New Testament writings. We have the reflective mood of John's Gospel and the more prosaic atmosphere of Mark's. The fact that God is the author of the Bible means that God inspired not only the ideas expressed therein, but also the verbal expression of these ideas.

Because God is the author of the Bible, the same God who can neither deceive nor be deceived, the Bible is inerrant, that is to say, free from error. The inerrance of the Bible is an article of the Catholic faith. Of course, problems about the inerrancy of the Bible will arise, and each problem must be solved individually. Still, Biblical scholars have discovered certain general principles which are applicable to problems of inerrancy:

"*(a)* The words of the Bible are always true in the sense which the human author conveys by them, and only in this sense. One must master the patterns and speech of the biblical writers before one can be sure of what this sense is.

"*(b)* One must distinguish the fallible man from the infallible writer. The man may have erroneous beliefs which will certainly betray themselves at times. Inerrancy means that these are not affirmed, not that they are imperceptible.

"*(c)* Inerrancy must be understood in terms of customary human linguistic usage. The Bible uses popular nontechnical language, figures of speech, paradox, approximation, telescoped narrative, nonchronological narrative, inexact quotations, folklore, legend, myth. . . .

"*(e)* Inerrancy must be conceived in terms of literary forms.

"*(f)* Inerrancy must be conceived in terms of the personal style of the writers.

"*(g)* The writer does not always intend to speak of things as they are in themselves. Thus things are described according to their external appearance, common inaccurate designations are used, advice is given which is valid only in a particular context, the *argumentum ad hominem* is employed — in a word, all the realities of common discourse appear."[2]

All of which brings me to the question of understanding the Bible. How are we to get at its meaning? By my discussion of the inerrancy of the Bible, I have suggested the difficulty of understanding it. One must expect such difficulty, since the reader is trying to understand a body of literature that was composed by a host of different writers over the course of thirteen or fourteen centuries. Moreover, these writers wrote against a cultural and historical background quite different from our own. Still, I don't want to exaggerate the difficulty of understanding the Bible, since the authors were human beings like ourselves.

Of course, when it comes to understanding the Bible, one who is familiar with Hebrew and Greek, the original languages of the Bible, will have an advantage over those who are not

2 Reprinted with permission of Charles Sribner's Sons, an imprint of Macmillan Publishing Company, from *Dictionary of the Bible*, James L. Hastings, editor. Copyright 1963 by Frederick G. Grant and H.H. Rowley. Article on "Inspiration."

familiar with these languages. The average reader of the Bible will have to rely upon a good translation. In the American Catholic Church, a translation known as the New American Bible is widely used.

To get at the meaning of the Bible, one must study not only individual words, but especially the sentences in which the words occur, and also the larger literary units of which the sentences are a part. These larger units of discourse often bear little resemblance to modern Western literary forms; rather, the literary forms of the Bible belong to Near Eastern culture, and must therefore be studied in themselves and in comparison with the forms of other Near Eastern literature, with which they have numerous points of contact. Again the average reader of the Bible will have to rely on Biblical scholars to do this analysis, and the reader should buy a translation — such as the New American Bible — that contains notes and explanations.

Finally, I must say a word about the role of the Church in the interpretation of the Bible. The Bible is the book of the Church. It reflects the faith of the Church. The same Spirit, who inspired the Biblical authors, inspires the faith of the Church. The Spirit cannot contradict himself. The interpretation of the Bible which prevails in the Church is the interpretation of the Spirit himself.

QUESTIONS FOR REVIEW

1. Why did the Church accept certain books into the Bible and exclude others?
2. In what sense is God the author of the Bible?
3. How do the human authors of the Bible reveal themselves?
4. In what sense is the Bible inerrant?
5. How do we get at the meaning of the Bible?

CHAPTER 20

The Sacraments (I)
IN GENERAL

Today let us speak about the sacraments which are administered by the Church and are the privileged channels of God's graces and blessings.

A sacrament, as Catholics use the term, is a religious act which has been instituted or chosen by Jesus Christ to symbolize and effect the divine life of grace in the souls of men and women. The Catholic Church recognizes seven sacraments: baptism, confirmation, the Holy Eucharist, penance or the sacrament of reconciliation, the anointing of the sick, holy orders, and matrimony.

Baptism illustrates the definition of a sacrament very well. The Jews practiced religious or ceremonial washing long before Christ, but Christ gave this ceremonial washing a new significance. He directed his representatives to baptize or wash new disciples (Mt 28:19). This washing both signifies and brings about the cleansing of the soul from sin and the communication of God's life which Catholics call sanctifying grace (see Jn 3:5).

The sacraments derive their efficacy from Christ. They are efficacious only because they are rooted in the cross of Jesus. His atoning death made possible the new life of grace which is communicated to us in a privileged way by the sacraments. We cannot stand literally at the foot of the cross, for time and space prohibit us from doing so. However, the sacraments enable us to overcome the barriers of time and space and stand with Mary and the women on Calvary.

By his death on the cross Jesus stored up for us, as it were, a reservoir of life and grace; and the sacraments are the channels by which this saving flood reaches us. The grace of the sacramental life of the Church flows from Christ as fountainhead. This is basically what we mean when we say that the Church's sacraments were instituted by Christ.

It has always been the conviction of the Church that the seven sacraments go straight back historically to the words and deeds of Jesus Christ when he lived on this earth. I shall endeavor to point out the relevant passages in the New Testament when I discuss the sacraments individually.

Eastern Orthodox Christians also believe in seven sacraments. Protestants tend to recognize only two sacraments, baptism and the Holy Eucharist. It is true that these two sacraments are given greater prominence in the New Testament than the others — probably because they are rites of initiation; and the writings of the New Testament were composed largely for new converts and prospective converts. Therefore, this emphasis upon baptism and the Eucharist should not surprise us. But it should not lead us to neglect the other sacraments.

Why did Jesus institute seven sacraments? The reason is that the divine life which Jesus wished to share with us is so rich and manifold that one sacrament would not suffice. Seven sacraments were needed to symbolize and effect the life of grace with its multiple ramifications and consequences. Moreover, Jesus was a man of his times. He was a Jew who drew upon his personal religious heritage in giving form to his Church. He adopted the religious rites with which he and his Jewish contemporaries were familiar, giving them a new and richer significance. For example, the Jews employed baptism or ritual washing; they held a sacred meal called the Passover Supper; and they confessed their sins. Jesus took these well-known and time-honored practices and gave them a new, Christian significance. Thus, a variety of Christian sacraments came into existence.

As I have said, the Church has always believed that the sacraments are rooted in the very words and deeds of the historical Jesus. Therefore, the Church claims no right either to create or to suppress a sacrament or to alter the essential elements of an existing sacrament. Some might argue, for example, that one should substitute beer for wine in certain cultures, and rice for bread in others, when celebrating the Eucharist. The Church does not permit this. I must note once more that Jesus was a man of his own times; he was a Jew and his humanity was shaped by the Jewish culture in which he grew up. Therefore, the Church which he founded and the sacraments which he instituted will always bear the stamp of his Jewish heritage.

In the case of the sacraments, and so many other things too, God conveys his gifts to us through material things. He revealed his existence to the Gentile nations through the things he has made (Rm 1:19); he gave his only Son to us through the humanity of Jesus; he revealed his thoughts to us through the words of the Bible; and he shares his life with us through the material elements of the sacraments.

One must not regard the administration of the sacraments as the practice of magic. Those who believe in magic assume that the divinity in whom they believe is forced to act through the magic rite. What is given is given under duress. The Church, however, believes that God has freely chosen the sacramental rites as the channels of his grace, while the human minister remains fully subject to him at all times.

At the same time the Church recognizes that God can and does bestow his gifts even without the reception of the sacraments. For example, an adult can be "born again" of the Spirit even without the baptism of water, if he or she repents of sin and chooses to love God above all else. Even so, such a person must be baptized if he or she is aware of the obligation; and the sacraments remain the privileged channels of God's grace.

The fruitful reception of the sacraments depends upon the disposition of the recipient. The rites do not dispense grace after the manner of an automat. The sacraments achieve different effects in different people. Those who are well disposed, that is to say, repentant and obedient, benefit fully from the celebration. Others do not.

In each of the seven sacraments we can identify the matter, the form, and the minister.

The Church uses such things as water, oil, bread, wine, and even gestures to administer the sacraments. These things are called the matter of the sacraments.

The form consists of the words that accompany the use of the matter. The form renders the action sacred and specific. For example, a nurse can pour water on an infant to wash it or to cool it or to baptize it. If the nurse baptizes the child in case of an emergency, the form makes it clear what she is doing. The form is a prayer rooted in the Scriptures. It is not a theological statement; it is God's word applied to this particular sacramental action.

Finally, there must be a minister to carry out the sacramental action. In the case of baptism it is the minister who pours the water and recites the form. In the case of the Holy Eucharist it is the minister who consecrates the bread and wine. Lay people can administer baptism and matrimony; only an ordained minister can administer the other sacraments. When he or she administers a sacrament, the minister must have the intention of doing what the Church does. This intention can be present even in an unbeliever. For example, an unbelieving doctor or nurse could baptize an infant who is dangerously ill. It is still possible for the unbeliever to intend what the Church does.

On this occasion I have spoken about the seven sacraments of the Church in a general way. On future occasions I shall speak about the sacraments individually. But there is one other matter I must call to your attention. Sometimes Catholics speak of Christ as a sacrament, or they say that the Church is a sacrament. This manner of speaking is correct in an analogous sense. In other words, there is a likeness between Christ and the Church on the one hand and the seven sacraments on the other. Just as the seven sacraments are the symbols and causes of God's grace in men and women, so Christ and the Church are symbols and causes of God's grace in his sons and daughters. Therefore, we can rightly apply the term sacrament to both Christ and the Church. Indeed Christ is the Great Sacrament because both the Church and the seven sacraments derive their efficacy from him.

QUESTIONS FOR REVIEW

1. What is a sacrament?
2. What are the names of the sacraments?
3. In what sense did Christ institute the sacraments?
4. Why did Christ institute more than one sacrament?
5. How do the sacraments bear the stamp of Jesus' Jewish heritage?
6. How do the sacraments differ from magical rites?
7. What is meant by the matter and form of the sacraments?
8. Who is the minister of the sacraments?
9. In what sense are Christ and the Church sacraments?

CHAPTER 21

The Sacraments (II)
BAPTISM AND CONFIRMATION

Now that I have spoken to you about the sacraments in general, I wish to consider the sacraments individually. First, then, baptism and confirmation.

The Gospel of Mark tells of the baptism of Jesus: "Jesus came from Nazareth of Galilee and was baptized in the Jordan by John. On coming up out of the water he saw the heavens being torn open and the Spirit, like a dove, descending upon him. And a voice came from the heavens, 'You are my beloved Son; with you I am well pleased' " (Mk 1:9-11). On this occasion Jesus instituted the sacraments of baptism and confirmation. The Head of the Church was baptized and anointed with the Spirit, so that the members of the Church might share the grace that flows from the Head.

Because Jesus personally was baptized with water, the Church has always considered water as essential to the rite of baptism. And because of the revelation of the Holy Trinity that marked the baptism of Jesus at the Jordan, the Church has always insisted upon a prayer-formula that mentions the Holy Trinity. An early formula for baptism is found at the end of Matthew's Gospel where Jesus said to the eleven: "Go, therefore and make disciples of all nations, baptizing them in the name of the Father, and of the Son, and of the Holy Spirit, teaching them to observe all that I have commanded you" (Mt 28:19-20).

The New Testament is quite explicit about the effect of the baptismal washing. Paul speaks of baptism as "the bath of rebirth and renewal by the Holy Spirit" (Ti 3:5). Our Lord assured Nicodemus in John's Gospel that "no one can enter the kingdom of God without being born of water and Spirit" (Jn 3:5).

Through baptism therefore, one is born again. The Christian receives a new life, different from the natural life of the body. The transformation that takes place is as striking as if a corpse in a funeral parlor were suddenly to sit up and begin to talk because he or she had begun to live a new life. This life, which Catholics call sanctifying grace, is nothing less than a created sharing in the life of God himself. Unquestionably an adult can be born again by repentance and conversion; but he or she is not dispensed from the obligation of being baptized if one is aware of it.

Because one receives the new life of sanctifying grace through baptism, baptism remits original sin. Essentially original sin is the privation of sanctifying grace in newborns as the result of Adam's sin. Baptism supplies this privation. It is for this reason that Catholics baptize infants.

However, Catholics do not baptize infants indiscriminately. Unless the child is in danger of death, an infant should be baptized only when the parents promise to raise their child as a Catholic. So that they can keep this promise, the parents and sponsors of a child who is to be baptized should be properly instructed about the nature of this sacrament and the obligations attached to it. An infant should be baptized within the first weeks after birth. If parents are unwilling to raise their child as a Catholic, then the baptism should be put off.

While parents and sponsors present an infant for baptism, adults must present themselves for the sacrament. They must have the intention to be baptized, be instructed in the truths of the Catholic religion and be sorry for their sins. To prepare adults for baptism, the Church has developed what is called a catechumenate. While converts in the earliest days of the Church were baptized immediately upon their profession of faith, the catechumenate soon came into existence. In the catechumenate prospective Christians were instructed, tested in their sincerity and desire, and initiated step by step into the Christian religion. Hippolytus of Rome, who lived in the third century, tells of a three year catechumenate. However, the catechumenate fell into disuse somewhat later as more and more Christians were baptized as infants. Since the Second Vatican Council in the early 1960's, the catechumenate has been restored to prominence as a means of leading converts to the faith and sharing in the Catholic community.

There is a dispute among Christians concerning the method of baptism. Should a candidate for baptism be immersed in water or should the minister simply pour water over his head? Certain evangelical Churches practice immersion only, while many other Christians accept the validity of both immersion and infusion. It seems that the apostolic Church accepted the validity of baptism by infusion too. We are told in the Acts of the Apostles, for example, that three thousand people received the message of Peter when he preached in Jerusalem on the first Pentecost. They were baptized and added to the Church on that day (Ac 2:41). In view of the scarcity of water in Jerusalem, it seems that baptism must have been conferred by infusion or even sprinkling on that occasion. In any event the Catholic Church baptizes either by immersion or infusion. This second method is widely used because of its practicality.

The sacrament of confirmation reposes upon the promise of Jesus to send another Advocate (Jn 14:16) who would teach the disciples everything (Jn 14:26), who would bear witness to Jesus and enable the disciples to bear witness to him (Jn 15:26-27). This promise was fulfilled when the Holy Spirit descended upon the apostles at the feast of Pentecost (Ac 2:1-4). At that moment they were transformed into eloquent and fearless witnesses to their divine Master. The descent of the Holy Spirit upon the apostles is the prototype of Christian confirmation. We read that the apostles in turn gave the Spirit by imposing their hands on the recipient (Ac 8:14-17). Yet I hasten to add that the gift of the Spirit is not tied to the external rite of confirmation. God can and did impart the Holy Spirit independently of the sacrament (Ac 10:44-46).

Four points remain to be made.

First, confirmation is a sacrament distinct from baptism; it is not merely a solemn renewal of baptism. Confirmation is an integral part of Christian initiation. The proper effect of confirmation is the gift of the Spirit in a special way and strength to become a witness to Christ by word and deed. This strength has been represented catechetically by metaphors like these: baptism makes us citizens, confirmation makes us soldiers; baptism gives us a new birth, confirmation makes us spiritual adults. We see, therefore, that baptism is intrinsically oriented to confirmation which we are expected to receive in due time to complete our initiation into the Church. Without baptism, however, we cannot receive any other sacrament, for baptism is the door to the Church.

A second point concerns the external rite of confirmation. Neither by his word nor by his example did Our Lord set the external rite of confirmation. Therefore, the Church has felt free to confer the gift of the Spirit by a variety of external rites: imposition of hands as in the Acts of the Apostles, anointing with oil as in the later ages of the Church, or both.

A third point is that both baptism and confirmation (and holy orders too) impress a spiritual and indelible character or seal upon the soul. The character of baptism is believed to configure a baptized person to Christ, while the character of confirmation is the seal of the Holy Spirit. The Biblical foundation of the sacramental character is the "seal" of God with which the elect are marked (Rv 7:2-8). Catholics have come to associate the character with the fact that neither baptism nor confirmation can be repeated. The character or seal remains even if the Christian loses the life of grace conferred and enhanced by baptism and confirmation. In every case the character reminds the Christian of the duty to possess the life of grace and also offers it.

A fourth and final point. The ordinary minister of baptism is a bishop, priest, or deacon. However, in case of necessity, anyone can baptize simply by pouring ordinary water on the forehead of the person to be baptized while saying at the same time: "I baptize you in the name of the Father, and of the Son, and of the Holy Spirit." The ordinary minister of confirmation is a bishop, but in some circumstances, as in danger of death, a priest may also administer the sacrament.

Now we are in a position to offer some definitions. Baptism is the sacrament by which we are freed from our sins, reborn as children of God, configured to Christ by an indelible mark, and incorporated into the Church. Confirmation is the sacrament through which the life of grace is enhanced in the soul and we are sealed by the Holy Spirit so that we may be dedicated witnesses to Christ.

The culmination of Christian initiation is the sacrament of the Eucharist. More about the Holy Eucharist the next time.

QUESTIONS FOR REVIEW

1. When did Jesus institute baptism and confirmation?
2. What is the external rite of baptism?
3. What are the effects of baptism?

4. Why should infants be baptized?
5. When should adults be baptized?
6. What is the catechumenate?
7. What is the effect of confirmation?
8. What is the external rite of confirmation?
9. What is meant by the character or seal of baptism and confirmation?
10. Who is the minister of baptism? Of confirmation?

CHAPTER 22

The Sacraments (III)
THE HOLY EUCHARIST

On the last occasion I spoke to you about baptism and confirmation. Now I wish to speak to you about the Holy Eucharist.

Jesus instituted the Holy Eucharist at the Last Supper on the night before he died. While he was eating with his apostles, "[Jesus] took bread, said the blessing, broke it, and gave it to them, and said, 'Take it; this is my body.' Then he took a cup, gave thanks, and gave it to them, and they all drank from it. He said to them, 'This is my blood of the covenant, which will be shed for many' " (Mk 14:22-24). Finally, Jesus enjoined his apostles to do what he had done in memory of him (Lk 22:19; 1 Cor 11:25). It is the conviction of Catholics that what Jesus did at the Last Supper is repeated in every Mass in obedience to this command.

The New Testament relates the account of the Last Supper in the Gospels of Matthew (26:26-29), Mark (14:22-24), and Luke (22:14-20), and the First Letter of Paul to the Corinthians (11:23-25). The language of these four writings, and that of John's Gospel where Jesus promised the Holy Eucharist (6:53-58), leaves no room for mere symbolism.

The manner in which the bread and wine become the body and blood of Christ is indeed a mystery of faith; but the true, real, and substantial presence of the body and blood may not be doubted. The wondrous change of elements is called transubstantiation. Transubstantiation means that the substance, or underlying reality, of bread and wine is converted by divine power into the very body and blood of Christ. After the consecration of the bread and wine, the appearances of bread and wine remain visually and chemically. In other words, the sign value of the table elements is preserved; but the substance of bread and wine has been changed into the body and blood of Christ.

Against this background, we understand that the Holy Eucharist directs our attention to the past, the present, and the future.

First, the Holy Eucharist directs our attention to the past. The Holy Eucharist recalls the Last Supper which Our Lord ate with his apostles. On that occasion Jesus shed his blood sacramentally, for the cup contained the blood of Jesus, the blood of the covenant, to be poured out on behalf of many (Mk 14:24). The Holy Eucharist recalls the physical death of Christ on Calvary. The separate consecration of the bread and wine symbolizes the actual separation of his body and blood on Calvary. The Holy Eucharist is the memorial of Christ's passion and death, a memorial which he himself left us. Our regular celebration of the Eucharist is explained, partially at least, by our desire to be ever mindful of Our Lord's passion and death and to share in its fruits in ever greater measure.

The Holy Eucharist also directs our attention to the present. The Holy Eucharist contains the whole Christ, body and blood, soul and divinity, truly, really, and substantially. Christ becomes our food. Not that we are cannibals, for Christ becomes our food under the appearances of bread and wine. When we receive the body and blood of Christ in Holy Communion, we achieve a closer union with Our Lord and a more fervent love of God and neighbor; we share more fully in God's life through sanctifying grace; we are preserved from sin, the most dreadful evil of all; and we are strengthened in the practice of good works. Our common participation in the Eucharistic meal and sacrifice is a symbol of our union with one another. Just as a family and friends share a meal, so we, the family and friends of God, share the Holy Eucharist. In these circumstances, envy, contention, quarreling, and hostility have no place.

Finally, the Holy Eucharist directs our attention to the future. It is the last sacrament we shall receive prior to our death. We are encouraged to receive Holy Communion frequently, even daily, in the course of our lives. Then, at the approach of death, we should receive the sacrament in the form of Viaticum as a provision for the journey. Holy Viaticum is not to be delayed too long, so that we may receive it while we are fully conscious.

What is more, the Holy Eucharist directs our attention to the future spiritual banquet in the kingdom of heaven. The New Testament often speaks of the kingdom of heaven in terms of a banquet. Our Lord said on one occasion: "Many will come from the east and the west, and will recline with Abraham, Isaac, and Jacob at the banquet in the kingdom of heaven" (Mt 8:11). At the Last Supper Our Lord promised the apostles that they would eat and drink at the table in his kingdom (Lk 22:30). Our eating and drinking at the table of the Eucharist is a symbol of the heavenly banquet. Indeed it is a pledge of future glory: "Whoever eats my flesh and drinks my blood," Jesus said, "has eternal life, and I will raise him on the last day" (Jn 6:54).

So the Holy Eucharist points to the past, the present and the future. All that I have said in this respect is captured by that lovely short antiphon recited or sung by Catholics in honor of the Holy Eucharist: "O holy banquet, in which Christ is received, the memory of his passion is renewed, the soul is filled with grace, and there is given to us a pledge of future glory!" I can offer no better idea of the Holy Eucharist than the one expressed by these few verses.

If the Holy Eucharist is the memorial of Christ's passion and death, the reason is that it is a sacrifice too. At the Last Supper Christ shed his blood sacramentally. On that occasion Jesus referred to his blood as the blood of the covenant which would be shed for many (Mk 14:24). This is sacrificial language. Such language shows that Jesus thought of the Last Supper as a sacrifice, as a sacramental or symbolic anticipation of his death on Calvary. Catholics think of the Holy Eucharist as a sacrifice too, for it is the renewal of the Last Supper in obedience to the command of Christ. In the Eucharistic sacrifice or Mass Christ renews the offering of himself to the Father. "The Mass is the sacrifice of the New Law in which Christ, through the ministry of priests, offers himself to God in an unbloody manner under the appearances of bread and wine."[1]

There is, of course, an important difference between the sacrifice of the cross and the sacrifice of the Mass. The manner in which the sacrifice is offered is different. On the cross Christ physically shed his blood and was physically slain, while in the Mass there is no physical shedding of blood nor physical death, because Christ can die no more. Moreover, on the cross Christ merited and satisfied on our behalf, while in the Mass he applies to us the merits and satisfaction of his death on the cross.

Christ is the principal priest of every Mass, for in every Mass Christ renews the offering of himself to the Father. Under Christ, only a validly ordained priest can consecrate the bread and wine. Still, all the faithful are called upon to participate in the celebration, each in his or her own way according to the diversity of roles.

1 *A Catechism of Christian Doctrine*, no. 3, Confraternity of Christian Doctrine, 1949, quest. 357.

In view of the nature of the Mass and its place in the Catholic tradition, it is no wonder that the Church obliges Catholics to attend Mass every Sunday and holy day of obligation. What is more, all the faithful, who have made their first Holy Communion, are obliged to receive Holy Communion at least once a year during the Easter season. Of course, the faithful are invited to receive Holy Communion more often, even daily, when they attend Mass. However, a person who is conscious of grave sin is not to receive the body and blood of Christ without prior sacramental confession, lest he or she eat and drink unworthily unto condemnation (1 Cor 11:27-32). One who is to receive the Holy Eucharist must abstain from food and drink, with the exception of water and medicine, for at least one hour before Holy Communion. Those who are old or sick, as well as those who take care of them, may receive the Holy Eucharist even if they have taken something during the previous hour. Even if they have received Holy Communion on the same day, those who are in danger of death are strongly urged to receive again.[2]

The reception of Holy Communion completes the initiation of the adult Christian into the Church, but the bread from heaven should nourish us all the days of our lives.

2 *Code of Canon Law*, cc. 916-921; 1246-1247.

QUESTIONS FOR REVIEW

1. When and how did Jesus institute the Holy Eucharist?
2. What is meant by transubstantiation?
3. How does the Holy Eucharist symbolize the death of Christ on Calvary?

4. How is Christ present in the Holy Eucharist?
5. What are the effects of Holy Communion?
6. How does the Holy Eucharist point to the future?
7. What is the Holy Eucharist?
8. In what sense is the Holy Eucharist a sacrifice?
9. What are the rules for fasting before the reception of Holy Communion?

CHAPTER 23

The Sacraments (IV)
PENANCE AND ANOINTING OF THE SICK

Today I wish to speak to you about penance and the anointing of the sick, the two sacraments of healing.

It is fitting that those who have been configured to Christ in baptism, sealed by the Holy Spirit in confirmation, and nourished by the body and blood of Christ in the Holy Eucharist should sin no more. Sad to say, none of us is completely faithful to our high calling, and we fail in great and small matters by sinning. Just as we need a physician to treat bodily illness, so we need a healer to treat the spiritual illness inflicted by sin. Christ is our healer in the sacrament of penance and the sacrament of the sick.

In the sacrament of penance or reconciliation, the sinner obtains the forgiveness of post-baptismal sins from Christ through the absolution of the priest. Catholics see the genesis of the sacrament of penance in the events of the first Easter day. On that occasion, Jesus appeared to his disciples as they gathered in a locked room. He showed them his hands and his side; and then, "He breathed on them and said to them, 'Receive the Holy Spirit. Whose sins you forgive are forgiven them, and whose sins you retain are retained' " (Jn 20:22-23).

By this striking action and by such clear words Jesus communicated the power to forgive sins to the apostles and their legitimate successors.

This calls our attention to the reality of sin. Jesus himself forgave sins, and he shared his power to forgive sins with others; therefore, there are sins to be forgiven. In some quarters there is a tendency to deny human responsibility for sin. Surely, some say, men and women do evil things. They can be cruel, destructive, and totally self-seeking. However, for various psychological reasons, they are not responsible for the evil they do. Our Lord did not share this attitude. He recognized the existence of sin and provided for its forgiveness.

Jesus provided a remedy for personal sins in the sacrament of penance. Do we Catholics realize what a blessing we have in this sacrament? Several years ago I addressed a group of Protestant ministers about some changes in the Catholic Church. In the course of the discussion that followed, one minister asked me, "Do Catholics still go to confession?" Then he added somewhat wistfully, "I wish I could go to confession. I wish I could approach someone in confidence to confess my sins and be assured of God's forgiveness." His remarks on that occasion made a deep impression upon me. It is an immense and immediate consolation for the sinner to be able to approach a living, accessible, and accredited representative of Christ for the forgiveness of sins. The need to confess one's sins is deeply imbedded in the human spirit.

Having said this, I hasten to add that God can and does forgive sins even outside the sacrament of reconciliation. If one repents of sin and turns to God as the supreme good, then his or her sins are forgiven at that moment. Even so, the repentant sinner must confess his or her sins to the minister of the Church, lest one be guilty of self-deception and be deprived of the judgment of the minister. Some believe that conversion, to be truly effective, requires reflection and the verbal articulation of guilt in a specific manner. Furthermore, by approaching the minister of the Church, the repentant sinner makes visible his or her reconciliation with the Church which has been injured by the sins.

The penitent sinner must do three things to receive the forgiveness of sins in the sacrament of penance.

First, he or she must be sorry for his or her sins. Sorrow for sin is the central act of the penitent who seeks reconciliation. Sorrow for sin includes remorse for having offended God, repudiation of the sins committed, and the firm intention to amend one's life. To confess one's sins without sorrow for them is merely to catalogue them, not to be freed from them.

Second, the penitent sinner must confess his or her sins to a priest, the only minister of the sacrament of penance. Serious sins, also known as mortal sins, *must* be confessed according to their kind and number. Only in this way can the confessor understand the penitent's condition. Lesser sins, often called venial sins, *may* be confessed; indeed, the confession of them is a powerful aid toward spiritual growth. (I shall say more about mortal and venial sins at another time.)

It is well-known that the Church absolutely forbids the confessor to violate the seal of confession, that is to say, to reveal in any way or for any reason what the penitent has confessed.

Third, the penitent sinner must accept the satisfaction, also called by the name "penance," which is assigned by the confessor. One has done evil by sinning; now one is assigned some good to do, often a simple good work or prayer. The confessor is directed to impose a salutary and suitable penance in keeping with the nature and number of sins committed, but in every case he must bear in mind the condition of the penitent.

Indulgences fulfill much the same purpose as the penance or satisfaction assigned by the confessor after the confession of sins. An indulgence is the remission in whole or in part of the temporal punishment due to a sin which has already been forgiven. Every sin merits temporal punishment of some kind. To gain the remission of the temporal punishment due to sin in whole or in part, one may perform a good work to which the Church, insofar as it can, attaches the satisfaction of Christ and the saints. In this way one can gain an indulgence.

The three acts of the penitent — sorrow, confession of sins, and acceptance of the penance — are called the matter of the sacrament of penance. When the confessor is satisfied that the penitent has elicited these acts in good faith, as far as he can judge, he imparts absolution. In the name of Christ the priest forgives the sinner. This declaration of forgiveness is the form of the sacrament.

Now I wish to turn my attention to the anointing of the sick, more commonly called extreme unction in the past. The anointing of the sick is the sacrament which is conferred upon those who are dangerously ill by anointing them with oil and using the appropriate words, so that the Lord will heal them spiritually and perhaps physically. As sin besets the pilgrim Church, so do illness and death, the consequences of sin.

We read that Jesus summoned the Twelve and sent them out, two by two. "They drove out many demons, and they anointed with oil many who were sick and cured them" (Mk 6:13). Healing was part of the disciples' ministry, an extension of Jesus' own ministry. In the ancient world oil was regarded as a cure-all. In the hands of the servants of Christ the old cures acquired a new virtue. The power of God became available in common things to the faith of men and women.

Subsequently, James spoke about the anointing of the sick: "Is anyone among you sick? He should summon the presbyters of the Church, and they should pray over him and anoint [him] with oil in the name of the Lord, and the prayer of faith will save the sick person, and the Lord will raise him up. If he has committed any sins, he will be forgiven" (Jm 5:14-15).

Here one sees the bond between the two sacraments of healing. The sacrament of penance is meant to deal with sins committed after baptism, while the anointing of the sick is meant to deal with sickness and death which are the consequences of sin. The anointing of the sick enhances the life of grace in the soul; it helps one to bear his or her serious illness; it prepares those who are to die of their illness for the glory of the life to come; and it affords physical healing when it is good for the soul. In the latter case, it is no substitute for the doctor, but it does provide aid at a more profound, mystical level.

According to the passage in the Letter of James which I have just quoted, a person can receive the forgiveness of sins through this sacrament. Catholics understand this to mean that one who is unable to confess his sins, perhaps because he is unconscious, can still be forgiven through this sacrament, provided he is sorry for his sins.

So, those who have reached the use of reason, who experience serious illness or injury, including serious debility from old age, should receive this sacrament from a priest, especially from their own pastor. The sacraments are for the living. Hence, the dead are not to be anointed.

QUESTIONS FOR REVIEW

1. When did Jesus institute the sacrament of penance or reconciliation?
2. How can sins be forgiven apart from this sacrament?
3. What must the penitent do to receive this sacrament?
4. What is an indulgence?
5. What is the “form” of the sacrament of penance?

6. Where are there references to the anointing of the sick in the New Testament?
7. What are the effects of the sacrament of anointing?
8. When does this sacrament forgive sins?
9. Who may receive this sacrament?

CHAPTER 24

The Sacraments (V)
HOLY ORDERS AND MATRIMONY

Today I wish to speak to you about the two sacraments of vocation, that is to say, about holy orders and matrimony. Five of the sacraments are offered to *all* the followers of Christ. But these two sacraments are intended for only *some* of the followers of Christ.

Our Lord and Savior Jesus Christ is the great high priest of the New Testament. As a priest, he offered himself as a sacrifice for sin on the cross of Calvary, a sacrifice that he anticipated at the Last Supper when he shed his blood sacramentally. Jesus took a cup at the Last Supper and said to the Twelve: "Drink from it, all of you, for this is my blood of the covenant, which will be shed on behalf of many for the forgiveness of sins" (Mt 26:27-28). That same sacrifice was to be offered repeatedly in the Church as the sacrifice of the Mass. "Do this in memory of me," Jesus told his apostles at the Last Supper (Lk 22:19; 1 Cor 11:25). In this way, Christ established the sacrament of holy orders. Christ appointed individuals to consecrate, offer, and administer his body and blood. The sacrament of holy orders is centered on this.

It is the belief of the Catholic Church, based upon the

teaching of the New Testament, that the priesthood of Christ is shared by all the members of the Church, although in different ways. The official position of the Catholic Church on this matter was stated by the Second Vatican Council (1962-65):

"Although they differ essentially and not only in degree the common priesthood of the faithful and the ministerial or hierarchical priesthood are nonetheless interrelated. Each of them in its own way is a participation in the one priesthood of Christ. The ministerial priest, that is to say, the ordained priest, by the sacred power he enjoys, teaches and rules the priestly people. Acting in the person of Christ, he effects the Eucharistic sacrifice and offers it to God in the name of all the people. But the faithful, in virtue of their royal priesthood, join in the offering of the Holy Eucharist. They exercise their priesthood too by the reception of the sacraments, by prayer and thanksgiving, by the witness of a holy life, self-denial, and active charity."[1]

A bishop confers the sacrament of holy orders when he lays his hands on the head of the recipient and recites the consecratory prayer proper to each ordination. This laying on of hands and consecratory prayer are the matter and form of the sacrament. However, one can share in the sacrament of holy orders on a threefold level, according as one is ordained bishop, priest or deacon.

Bishops hold the fullness of the priesthood, and, according to the faith of Catholics, they are the successors of the original apostles. Bishops are the teachers and shepherds of their flocks. The chief teacher and shepherd of the universal Church is the bishop of Rome, who, by that very fact, is the successor to Peter, the prince of the apostles, and the rock upon whom the Savior built his Church (Mt 16:18). The other bishops are the teachers and shepherds of various portions

1 Constitution on the Church, no. 10.

of the Lord's flock called dioceses. Some bishops serve as auxiliaries to those who have the care of a diocese.

Priests also receive the sacrament of holy orders. They are united to their bishop in priestly dignity. They cooperate with their bishop in his work. They take his burdens and duties upon themselves. Priests make the bishop present in every smaller unit of a diocese called a parish. Priests are the teachers and shepherds of a parish.

With relatively few exceptions, bishops and priests of the Catholic Church do not marry, so that they can devote themselves to their ministry with the greatest possible freedom.

Finally, there are the deacons of the Church. They too receive the sacrament of holy orders. Those who plan to remain deacons throughout their lives may be married. While deacons are not empowered to celebrate the Holy Eucharist, forgive sins, and anoint the sick, they are at the disposal of the bishop in other matters. They provide for the sick and poor, take Holy Communion to the sick confined to their homes, confer baptism, witness marriages, preach the gospel, preside at funerals, and assist the priest in divine worship.

The 1970's raised a new issue: Can women be admitted to holy orders along with men? The fundamental question is this: Was it the will of Christ that only men be called to ordained ministry as a matter of principle? Those who oppose the ordination of women in principle feel that the tradition of excluding them derives from the mind of Christ. That is Pope John Paul II's view of the matter, and incidentally mine as well. The Catholic Church, which was founded by Christ and is guided by the Holy Spirit, has consistently understood and taught that Christ called only men to holy orders.

Both sexes are called to share the second sacrament of vocation, matrimony: and sexuality is a central feature of the sacrament. The union of husband and wife has been raised by our divine Savior to the level and dignity of a sacrament. The sacrament enhances the life of grace within the spouses, and it helps them to fulfill their mutual responsibilities. When did Jesus make marriage a sacrament? The matter is disputed, but he probably did so when he restored the pristine permanence of marriage after Moses had permitted the Jews to write a bill of divorce and dismiss their wives (Mt 5:31-32; Mk 10:1-12). The sacrament of matrimony is administered by the contracting parties, each of whom confers the sacrament on the other. According to the present legislation of the Church, a Catholic can contract a valid marriage only in the presence of the Church's minister and two witnesses.

Reflecting upon the nature of Christian marriage, Paul spoke of marriage as a symbol of the union between Christ and his Church. Yes, the husband is head of the home, just as Christ is head of the Church; but the husband must love his wife even as Christ loved the Church (Ep 5:22-33). When a husband's love for his wife reflects Christ's love for his Church, then the wife is raised to a new dignity in Christianity. She is a true partner in marriage, and her subjection implies no servitude or debasement.

The union between husband and wife is a permanent one. Jesus said: "From the beginning of creation, 'God made them male and female. For this reason a man shall leave his father and mother [and be joined to his wife], and the two shall become one flesh.' So they are no longer two but one flesh. Therefore what God has joined together, no human being must separate" (Mk 10:6-9). In this connection I think of the lady who had been married fifty years. "Were you ever tempted to divorce your husband?" she was asked. "Divorce, never!" she replied, "but murder, many times." Only death can end a valid, sacramental, and consummated marriage.

Along with a deep concern to preserve the permanence of marriage, the Church has always tried to offer support and compassion to those Catholics whose marriages have failed and ended in divorce. As long as they do not remarry, divorced Catholics are permitted to receive the sacraments and should be fully accepted by other Catholics. Those Catholics who have remarried after a civil divorce, however, are excluded from receiving Holy Communion. Even then they should continue to pray, attend Mass, and remain as active as they can in the Church community.

By its very nature marriage is oriented toward begetting and rearing children. New life is the fruit of marriage. It is true that fruitfulness is sometimes absent. The sterility of one partner does not necessarily invalidate marriage. Even a virginal marriage, if agreed upon by both partners, can be a valid one. Yet it must be possible for the partners to be sexually active in a human way. Impotence excludes one from marrying. And homosexual marriages, by their very nature, are invalid, since the fundamental nature of sex demands the male-female union.

It is up to husband and wife to determine the number of children they wish to bring into the world. They will make this decision after taking into account their state of health, financial resources, the difficulty of previous births, and other considerations. Still, not all means of limiting the size of one's family are legitimate. Abortion and artificial contraception are illegitimate means of limiting the size of one's family. Natural family planning methods, though, are legitimate and effective.

Preparation is generally necessary for the success of any important undertaking, including marriage. To prepare for a holy and happy marriage, Catholics should pray to the Holy Spirit and consult their parents for guidance in the choice of a partner. They should practice the virtues, especially chastity, and receive the sacraments of penance and Holy Eucharist frequently.

QUESTIONS FOR REVIEW

1. When did Jesus institute the sacrament of holy orders?
2. What is the difference between the priesthood of the laity and the ordained priesthood?
3. How does a bishop confer holy orders?
4. What is the difference between bishops, priests, and deacons?
5. Why can't women be ordained?
6. When did Jesus institute the sacrament of matrimony?
7. Who are the ministers of the sacrament?
8. What is the symbolism of Christian marriage?
9. Why is Christian marriage a permanent union?
10. What is the place of divorced Catholics in the Church?
11. How should husband and wife determine the size of their family?
12. How can Catholics prepare for a holy and happy marriage?

CHAPTER 25

THE LAST THINGS

I wish to speak to you at this point about those things which await the individual at the end of his or her life and at the end of human history. Generally Christians think of four last things that await the individual: death, judgment, heaven or hell.

Death is a visible and undeniable reality. No matter how many ways a person may achieve success in this world, ultimately he or she must lose: he or she must die. During the past century, human beings have made themselves the masters of their environment to a greater degree than many thought possible. They have conquered the land, sea, air, and space with their machines and devices. To some extent they have even conquered time by prolonging the span of life. Yet, despite these huge strides forward, human beings — rich or poor, wise or ignorant, sinner or saint — must ultimately lose: they must lie down and die.

Death is a fact and will continue to be so. The only defense that the carnal man has worked out against the grim reality of death is to fight it tooth and nail when the need arises, and between bouts to forget the whole unpleasant matter.

The attitude of the Christian is profoundly different. For the Christian death means going to be with our Father in heaven. It means sharing the life, light, and joy of the heavenly kingdom. Death is a friend. We call this world the land of the living, but it would be more correct to call it the land of the dying. When death comes, the Christian believes, we pass out of the land of the dying into the land of the living. In this world we are journeying not to the sunset, but to the sunrise. Death is the entrance into glory. For the believing Christian, the worst and last of life's horrors turns out to be a harmless bogey. Yes, Christians weep when they are separated from loved ones through death, but through the tears they glimpse the glory.

It is the faith of Catholics that each one is judged immediately after death. This judgment is called the particular judgment. By this judgment the soul is assigned a place among the saved or damned. The decision of this judgment is final and will not be reversed. The body of one who dies is placed in the ground after death. There it awaits the resurrection. By the resurrection of the body is meant that the bodies of all men and women will rise from the earth at the end of the world and be reunited with their souls, never more to be separated. No one knows when the world will end. The Scriptures suggest certain general signs that will signal the end of the world, but the exact moment remains unknown. The bodies of the saved will rise to share in the glory of the soul. The bodies of the damned will also rise to share in the eternal punishment of the soul.

The doctrine of the particular judgment excludes the theory of reincarnation, which teaches that the soul passes from one body to another for an undefined period of time, that death is not the end of our probation. However, the finality of the particular judgment excludes this. Once judgment has taken place, the soul of a person cannot be reborn in a new body.

Who will be rewarded in heaven? Those who have died as friends of God; they have kept his commandments and repented of their sins; and, if necessary, they have been purified in purgatory. (More about purgatory in a moment.) In heaven, we shall be with God our Father.

What it means to be with our heavenly Father is suggested to me by a story that I heard from a priest-friend. He and a Jewish rabbi had gone to Palestine some years ago to dig in some old Biblical ruins. The rabbi had left his wife and two children behind because the digging party was going to work in some remote areas. The party returned home after several months. The wife and children of the rabbi met him as he entered the airport in New York. The children rushed up to him, held him close, buried their faces in his coat, and said over and over again, "Father! Father! Father!" The scene was one of great tenderness and emotion.

In heaven we shall be with God our Father. We shall see God face to face and share forever in his glory and happiness. We shall rejoice in the company of Our Savior, the Blessed Virgin Mary, and the angels and saints. We shall be reunited with our families and friends. There is no sorrow or pain in heaven; our joy will be complete.

Who will be punished in hell? Those who die as enemies of God, who have not kept his commandments, nor repented of their sins. In hell the damned are deprived of the vision of God and suffer for all eternity. Who can appreciate what it means to be deprived of the vision of God? We human beings were made to rejoice in the presence of God. Perhaps you will recall the words of Augustine, a great saint: "Our hearts were made for thee, O God, and they will not rest until they rest in thee." In other words, just as our bodies hunger for food, just as our lungs seek air, so our hearts yearn for the presence of God. In hell this yearning of the human heart will be forever frustrated. This frustration will be one of the principal torments of hell. Scripture describes the torments of hell in terms of "fire" (Mt 25:41; Lk 16:24), "the gloom of darkness" (2 P 2:17), and "wrath and fury" (Rm 2:8). Regardless of how literal or figurative these images are, condemnation to hell is a catastrophe, a tragedy, of cosmic proportions. The doctrine of hell is immensely sobering, but it shows how seriously God takes human freedom and responsibility.

Who will be punished in purgatory? Those who die as friends of God without serious sins, yet are guilty of unrepented venial sin or have not fully satisfied for the temporal punishment due to sin. The main enterprise of the present life is to conform ourselves to Christ. We have made the fundamental decision to do so. But this decision must be carried out in time. It cannot be carried out at once by fiat for it is subject to the vacillation for which human nature is notorious. Each person proceeds at his or her own pace as he or she strives to be conformed to Christ. We need not be surprised if men and women experience varying degrees of success in this great task of life. Those who have not fully conformed themselves to Christ in the course of life are obliged to do so after death in purgatory.

A vivid suggestion of the Catholic doctrine of purgatory is found in the Second Book of Maccabees (12:42-46). There Judas, the Jewish leader, ordered sacrifices for dead soldiers that they might be loosed from their sins. The doctrine of purgatory is reflected in the worship of the early Church which offered prayers for the dead. Such prayers were inscribed on the walls of the catacombs. The Second Vatican Council encouraged Catholics to cultivate the memory of the dead and pray for them.[1] I must note, however, that purgatory will cease to be after the general judgment.

The general judgment will take place at the end of human history. The Lord Jesus will come in his majesty, and all the angels with him. He will sit on the throne of his glory, and all nations will be gathered before him (Mt 25:31-32). Then he will render to everyone according to his or her conduct (Mt 16:27). The general judgment at the end of the world will

1 Constitution on the Church, no. 50.

confirm the decision of the particular judgment at the end of one's life. The general judgment will vindicate the mercy, justice, and wisdom of God in the eyes of all. It often happens that the justice and wisdom of God are hidden from the eyes of human beings in the present world. Those who lead good lives frequently have many trials to endure, while those who transgress God's laws prosper. Many ask, "How can God permit such a state of affairs?" And so, in order that human beings may see that God is just, and may understand that in the next life, if not in this one, everyone receives what is due, there is a final or general judgment. At this judgment everything will be set right, and all evil will be removed from the kingdom of God.

QUESTIONS FOR REVIEW

1. What is the Christian attitude toward death?
2. What is the particular judgment?
3. Who are rewarded in heaven?
4. What are the rewards of heaven?
5. Who are punished in hell?
6. What are the punishments of hell?
7. Who must be purified in purgatory?
8. What is the purpose of the general judgment?

PART II

CATHOLIC PRACTICE

CHAPTER 26

THE GOAL OF LIFE

I am speaking to you about Catholic belief and practice. I have just completed my first series of talks dealing with the belief of Catholics. I spoke of God, the Supreme Being. In the one God there are three divine persons, Father, Son and Holy Spirit. God is the creator of all else besides himself, including angels and human beings. Human beings are composed of body and soul, enjoying free will and great control over their own lives. Abusing their freedom, the parents of the human race rebelled against their Maker, a rebellion that was and is aggravated by the sins of Adam's descendants. The result was a state of alienation between God and the human race.

However, God intervened in human history to win the rebels back to himself. He sent his only Son into the world as a sacrificial victim. The incarnate Son of God, whom we know as Jesus Christ, proclaimed the Father's forgiveness and summoned sinful human beings to conversion. At the same time, Jesus called men and women to share the life of Father, Son, and Holy Spirit, that is to say, to live on a new level of existence through the supernatural reality of grace.

To continue the proclamation of God's forgiveness and grace, Jesus established the Church, the people of God, under the leadership of Peter and the original apostles. Today that Church is known as the Catholic or Universal Church. The

Church proclaims the message of Jesus and administers his sacraments which are the privileged channels of the divine life of grace. To those who respond to the call delivered by his Son and the Church God promises a kingdom. This kingdom is called the kingdom of God in the Gospels of Mark and Luke or the kingdom of heaven in the Gospel of Matthew. We may say that the goal of life on this earth is to gain admission into the kingdom of God, the kingdom of heaven.

Jesus described God's kingdom, the kingdom of heaven, in some detail. Admission to the kingdom means joy, for on the day of reckoning, the master will say to each of his faithful servants, "Come, share your master's joy" (Mt 25:21). Jesus also described God's kingdom as life (Mk 9:43, 45) and light (Lk 16:8), and one finds in it the satisfaction of every pious desire (Mt 5:3-12). Jesus compared the kingdom to a treasure (Mt 13:44). One may sacrifice so great a good as marriage for the sake of the kingdom, for Jesus spoke approvingly of those who have freely renounced sex for the sake of the kingdom (Mt 19:12). In the kingdom of God, the kingdom of heaven, we hope to be completely filled by the glory of God as he wipes the tears from our eyes (Rv 7:17). In that kingdom we shall see God just as he is (1 Jn 3:2), and we shall be like him for all eternity and praise him unceasingly through Christ Our Lord. A person cannot turn away from God in heaven, since the goodness of God is seen too clearly and the happiness it entails is experienced too intensely to be rejected.

Complete and enduring happiness can be found only in the presence of God in heaven. It is not to be found in any created good, even though it may afford a limited measure of happiness for a time. The rich man may rejoice in his wealth; the successful woman, in the acclaim she receives. The politician may find satisfaction in the power she wields; the athlete, in his physical prowess. The hedonist may revel in his pleasures; and the scholar may find fulfillment in his learning. But all these things afford only a limited measure of happiness.

They are more or less transitory. They do not exclude unhappiness in other respects, and those who possess them may lack many another good thing, such as wisdom and health. Perfect happiness cannot be found in any created good which always leaves something to be desired. Perfect happiness can be found only in God, the universal good. The horizon of human beings is too broad, their appetites are too extensive to be satisfied with anything less. Our hearts are restless until they rest in God, as the great St. Augustine testified in his *Confessions* long ago.

For the Catholic, then, life is full of profound meaning. However, that meaning is not fully understood in terms of life on this earth. We are destined for fellowship with God and everlasting life in his kingdom. We are pilgrims on this earth traveling to our heavenly home. Such an understanding of the present life should govern our use of the things of this world. As St. Ignatius of Loyola (1491-1556), the founder of the Jesuits, wrote in his *Spiritual Exercises*: "We were created for a certain end. This end is to praise, to reverence, and to serve the Lord our God, and by this means to arrive at eternal salvation. All other beings and objects which abound upon this earth were created for our benefit and to be useful to us as means to our final end. Hence, we have the obligation to use, or to abstain from the use of, these creatures, according as they bring us nearer to that end, or tend to separate us from it."[1] We must desire and choose definitively in every matter what will lead us to the goal of our creation.

Needless to say, we may not be indifferent to the things of this world. As I remarked on another occasion, most Catholics seek the kingdom of God by their involvement in material and secular affairs. They are absorbed by family, social, and business concerns. They participate in the trades and professions. By their technical skills and cultural endowments they

1 First Principle or Foundation.

assist all human beings to benefit from created goods. By striving for a just social order they prepare the field of the world for the seed of the gospel. Still, Catholics will see all things in the light of eternity. They will ask themselves in every situation, "What does this mean for eternity?"

A clear idea of the goal of life is vitally important, for it determines how one lives. One who believes that God calls human beings to eternal happiness will obviously live differently than one who believes that death is the end of existence, that the present life affords the only opportunity of happiness.

All that I have said up to this point was put quite succinctly by the first two questions and answers in the Baltimore Catechism which I studied as a boy. The first question was: "Who made you?" And the answer was: "God made me." The second question was: "Why did God make you?" And the answer was: "God made me to know him, to love him, and to serve him in this world, and to be happy with him forever in heaven."

What then are we to do in order to achieve communion with God and everlasting life in heaven?

First, we must be born again. We are reborn primarily through the sacrament of baptism. We are reborn, in a sense, when we repent of our sins and turn to God. I have discussed this in more detail in my talk on baptism and penance. Such a rebirth is purely a gift of God.

Second, as adopted sons and daughters of God, redeemed by Christ and living on a new level of existence, adults must direct their actions toward God, the beginning and goal of human existence. I shall try to show how this is done in this second series of talks about Catholic practice. However, I may say briefly that adults achieve the goal of life through a life of love, that is to say, through obedience to God and service of neighbor, for love manifested in this way merits an eternal reward.

QUESTIONS FOR REVIEW

1. What is the goal of human life?
2. Can any created good provide perfect happiness?
3. What is the purpose of creatures other than ourselves?
4. How do we achieve the goal of human life?

CHAPTER 27

HUMAN ACTIONS

The fact that God calls human beings to everlasting life and happiness implies that they have the capacity to respond to the divine invitation. It is the clear teaching of Jesus and the Church that we respond to God's invitation through love of God and neighbor.

For example, on one occasion a scholar of the law put a question to Jesus: " 'Teacher, what must I do to inherit eternal life?' Jesus said to him, 'What is written in the law? How do you read it?' He said in reply, 'You shall love the Lord, your God, with all your heart, with all your being, with all your strength, and with all your mind, and your neighbor as yourself.' He replied to him, 'You have answered correctly; do this and you will live' " (Lk 10:25-28). Jesus then went on to tell the story of the Good Samaritan to explain what it means to love one's neighbor.

Jesus specified in greater detail the loving actions that lead to eternal life. A rich young man approached Jesus and said, " 'Teacher, what good must I do to gain eternal life?' He answered him, 'Why do you ask me about the good? There is only One who is good. If you wish to enter into life, keep the commandments.' He asked him, 'Which ones?' And Jesus replied, 'You shall not kill; you shall not commit adultery; you shall not steal; you shall not bear false witness; honor your father and your mother; and you shall love your neighbor as yourself' " (Mt 19:16-19). In other words, one gains eternal life through love of God and neighbor, a love that manifests itself by keeping the commandments.

In the Sermon on the Mount (Mt 5:1-7:28), Jesus appears as a new Moses, a new law-giver. Jesus tells us that he did not come to abolish the law or the prophets, but to fulfill them (Mt 5:17). He then goes on to proclaim new commandments about murder, adultery, divorce, and other matters which represent the fulfillment of the Mosaic Law. If we fulfill these commandments as Jesus requires, then our righteousness will surpass that of the scribes and Pharisees and we shall enter the kingdom of heaven (Mt 5:20).

Some have seen a conflict between the teaching of Jesus and that of Paul in this matter, because Jesus taught that we are saved from our sins and inherit eternal life by keeping the commandments, while Paul taught that we are saved by faith. For example, Paul states: "By grace you have been saved through faith" (Ep 2:8). However, we must understand that for Paul, faith means the acceptance of Christ. This acceptance is not merely an intellectual assent to the teaching of Christ, but a vital, personal commitment to Christ in all things. One manifests his or her basic commitment to Christ through deeds of love. So Paul writes: "In Christ Jesus, neither circumcision nor uncircumcision counts for anything, but only faith working through love" (Gal 5:6). That is why Paul continually exhorts his Christian converts to the practice of good deeds. I consider, therefore, that Jesus' teaching about love and keeping the commandments is consistent with Paul's teaching about commitment to Christ and doing good deeds.

James also writes about the necessity of a practical faith: "What good is it, my brothers, if someone says he has faith, but does not have works? Can that faith save him? If a brother or sister has nothing to wear and has no food for the day, and one of you says to them, 'Go in peace, keep warm, and eat well,' but you do not give them the necessities of the body, what good is it? So also faith of itself, if it does not have works, is dead" (Jm 2:14-17).

The Christian who lives a life of faith which expresses itself in love enjoys *freedom*. Paul teaches that the Christian enjoys freedom from sin (Rm 6:18-23), freedom from death, the inevitable companion of sin (1 Cor 15:56-57), freedom from concupiscence (Rm 7:3-35), and freedom from the observance of the Jewish law (Rm 7:1-6). No longer do these bonds impede the believer who is guided by the Spirit (Gal 5:18). Led by the Spirit of God, believers are sons and daughters of God who have not received a spirit of slavery, but a spirit of adoption (Rm 8:14-15).

However, freedom is not license. Christians are to place themselves at one another's service (Gal 5:13-14). Paul made himself the slave of all (1 Cor 9:19); in this he imitated Christ (1 Cor 11:1), the servant of all. All are equally free in Christ so that Christians are not distinguished by national, social, or racial characteristics (Gal 3:28).

A corollary of freedom is *responsibility*. The Bible holds men and women responsible for their actions. The prophets of Israel held prince and people responsible for the good or evil they had done. For example, the prophet Nathan spoke God's judgment to King David: "Now, therefore, the sword shall never depart from your house, because you have despised me and have taken the wife of Uriah to be your wife" (2 S 12:10). In the Book of Ezekiel we read: "Only the one who sins shall die. . . . The virtuous man's virtue shall be his own, as the wicked man's wickedness shall be his" (Ezk 18:20). Israel had been exiled, the prophets said, because it had failed in its responsibility to God (Jr 25:1-14).

The New Testament, too, holds men and women accountable for their actions. While God is good and creation is good, sin entered the world through one man. Human beings are partly, but really responsible for the evil that is present in the world (Rm 5:12). Paul thought that the Jewish law made the Israelites conscious of their responsibility to God, that it was a teacher given by God to instruct the Israelites about what to do and what not to do. It confronted them with a choice for or against God (Gal 3:19-26). The pagans were confronted by the same responsible choice, for the demands of the law were written in their hearts (Rm 2:15). The New Testament assigns responsibility for the death of the Son of God on the cross (Jn 19:11; Ac 3:13-14). All of this goes to show that men and women are responsible for what they do because they are free.

If one corollary of human freedom is responsibility, a second corollary is *reward and punishment.* The idea of reward and punishment is prominent in the Bible. God is an equitable master: he does not fail to give each one his or her due. God approves or disapproves the work of his servants. To be sure, there is a conception of collective responsibility in the Bible. The actions of some have significance for the whole group. The obvious example of solidarity in punishment is the story of Adam's fall in Genesis. And the obvious example of solidarity in reward is the common sharing in the salvific death and resurrection of Christ. Still, each person is responsible at every moment for his or her own destiny: the virtuous person shall surely live, while the wicked person shall surely die (Ezk 18:20). Jesus and his apostles sustained the traditional teaching of Israel about reward and punishment. At the end, Jesus said, the Son of Man will sit on his throne; and he will render to each one reward and punishment according to his works (Mt 25:31-46).

In conclusion, allow me to summarize the points I have made in this talk. The goal of life on this earth is eternal happiness with God in heaven. Adults achieve this through love of God and neighbor, manifested by keeping God's commandments. Our actions as human beings are characterized by freedom and responsibility, and they merit reward if they are good, and punishment if they are evil.

QUESTIONS FOR REVIEW

1. How do we achieve eternal life?
2. How are love of God and service of one's neighbor related to keeping the commandments?
3. In what sense is the Christian free?
4. Why are we responsible for our actions?
5. What is a further consequence of freedom and responsibility?

CHAPTER 28

THE MORAL LAW

God made us to know him, love him, and serve him in this life, and to be happy with him forever in heaven. Perfect happiness cannot be found in any created good which always leaves something to be desired. Perfect happiness can be found only in God, the universal good. Our hearts are restless until they rest in God.

As I showed in my previous talk, adults achieve eternal happiness in heaven through love of God and neighbor which is manifested by obedience to God's commandments and service to one's neighbor. Do this and you shall live. On future occasions I plan to specify in greater detail the demands of love where God and neighbor are concerned.

There are two things which help us to know the specific demands of love. They are the moral law and human conscience. The moral law is said to be the *objective* norm of conduct, and conscience is said to be the *subjective* norm of conduct. I shall try to explain what I mean by these statements. I will speak about the moral law now, and I will discuss conscience the next time.

A law is a measure dictated by reason and directed toward the common good; it stems from a competent legislator. Hence, a law is an exercise of good sense by a legislator who obliges a community to do such and such a thing. The purpose of the law is to secure the good of the society in which it prevails. A law that is harmful to society is not really a law at all. A law stems from a competent legislator whether authority is vested in an individual, such as a president, or in a group, such as a legislature. Of course, a law must be promulgated so that those subject to the law can know of its existence. The manner of promulgation is left up to the legislator.

The highest norm of human conduct is God's *eternal law*. When a builder constructs a house, he works according to a definite plan. The eternal law of God is similar to the plan of a builder. When God created the universe, he worked according to a plan. He executed the plan with a definite purpose in mind. God's plan established goals for his creatures and the means to achieve them. The determination of God to create and act according to a definite plan was eternal, although it is executed in time.

God's eternal plan as it governs human beings is called the *natural law*. God created human nature for a definite purpose. He endowed that nature with a natural tendency toward the goal he established for it, and he provided it with the resources to achieve it. When men and women act in accordance with human nature and its inherent characteristics and propensities, they act in accordance with the natural and eternal law of God: they act rightly. When they do not act in such a manner, they act wrongly.

Then there is another kind of divine law called *divine positive law*. This is the law which was directly and supernaturally revealed by God. As the Letter to the Hebrews put it: "In times past, God spoke in partial and various ways to our ancestors through the prophets; in these last days, he spoke to us through a son" (Heb 1:1-2). Speaking to his people through the prophets and his Son Jesus, God manifested his will for his subjects. In some instances, he reaffirmed the prescriptions of the natural law in order to clarify and certify them for all. Thus, he gave the Ten Commandments to the Israelites through

Moses. In other instances, he communicated the decisions of his divine will about the manner in which men and women were, and are, to serve him in the course of life. These decisions constitute the divine positive law in the strict sense.

We find the provisions of the divine positive law in the Bible especially. Under the Old Testament, God's will for the people was expressed by the Torah or Jewish law, which was closely connected with the covenant. God elected Israel as his chosen people, and he joined certain promises to his election. If the Israelites were to be the beneficiaries of these promises, they had to obey the law given by God through Moses. The law was inextricably bound up with the covenant. The law was a sacred obligation. The fate of society and the individual was thought to be determined by their attitude towards the law. The prophets recognized the authority of the Torah, the law, and rebuked the people when they violated it. After the exile (587-538 B.C.), the Jews placed the Torah at the center of their life. The law was considered to contain all knowledge, divine and human. The Pharisees developed an oral law to make the violation of the written law more difficult. Still, the prophets, such as Ezekiel (36:26-27) and Jeremiah (31:31-34), anticipated a new covenant and a new law, when the hearts of the people would finally come to obey the ordinances of God.

The new covenant was realized, Christians believe, in the activity and teaching of Jesus. According to the Gospels, Jesus himself observed the Torah or written law, but he rejected the oral law of the Pharisees. Jesus had come to fulfill the law and not to abolish it (Mt 5:17). He went on to say that whoever fulfills and teaches the commandments of the law shall be great in the kingdom of heaven (Mt 5:19). Ultimately Jesus reduced all the commandments of the law to two: love of God and love of neighbor. On these two commandments rest the whole law and the prophets (Mt 23:34-40). However, Jesus promulgated new provisions of the divine positive law such as those having to do with the Church, the sacraments, and the demands of Christian living.

The apostolic community continued to obey the Jewish law, but the admission of the Gentiles to the Christian community raised an important question. Were they to be bound by all the prescriptions of the Mosaic law? A plenary council at Jerusalem, with the support of Peter, James, and Paul, finally affirmed the freedom of the Gentile converts from the Jewish law (Ac 15:1-29).

Paul taught that a person is justified by faith in Jesus Christ and not by works of the law (Gal 2:16; Rm 3:28). This means that the ritual practices of Judaism were futile and that a person cannot merit his or her own reconciliation with God. What then was the purpose of the Mosaic law in the plan of salvation? It impressed upon the Jews their absolute need of the Savior. Once the Savior had come, the people no longer needed the law as a teacher. Still, the law continues to find its fulfillment in the great commandment of love (Gal 5:14). What about the Gentiles who were without the Mosaic law? They had a law written on their hearts, and they will be judged in accordance with that law (Rm 2:14-16). God's eternal power and divinity were known to the Gentiles by the things God has made (Rm 1:19-20).

Turning to the Gospel of John, we hear the words of Jesus: "Whoever has my commandments and observes them is the one who loves me. And whoever loves me will be loved by my Father, and I will love him and reveal myself to him" (Jn 14:21).

Having spoken about the divine positive law I must also mention two other kinds of law: Church law and civil law.

Church law is also called ecclesiastical law. Christ gave his Church the authority to make laws. This authority is sometimes described as the power to bind and loose. It is exercised in the Catholic Church by the Pope and ecumenical councils on behalf of the universal Church, and by bishops on behalf of their dioceses. The laws of fast and abstinence are examples of Church law.

Finally, there is *civil law*. Civil law aims at the common good of the community in which it prevails and not at the good of a few individuals only. Traffic and housing laws are examples of civil law. Civil authorities can pass laws which bind citizens in conscience, since civil authorities are representatives of God himself (Rm 13:1-2).

To summarize then what I have been saying: We achieve everlasting happiness with God in heaven through love of God and neighbor, that is to say, through obedience to God's commandments and service to one's neighbor. There are two things which help us to know what the specific demands of love are, what the commandments of God require. They are the moral law and the human conscience. The moral law is the *objective* norm of human conduct. It is the voice of God; it is the expression of God's will for human beings. Obedience to law is obedience to God.

More about conscience, the *subjective* norm of human conduct, on the next occasion.

QUESTIONS FOR REVIEW

1. What is the objective norm of human conduct?
2. What is the relationship between love and law?
3. What is a law?
4. What is the eternal law of God?
5. What is the natural law?
6. What is the divine positive law? Where is it to be found?
7. What is Church law?
8. What is civil law?

CHAPTER 29

CONSCIENCE

Two things help us to know what the specific demands of love are, what the commandments of God require. They are the moral law and human conscience. The moral law is the *objective* norm of human conduct. We may say that the moral law is the voice of God speaking to us about what is commanded and forbidden, what is right and wrong.

However, there is another voice which speaks to us about what is right and wrong. That voice is called conscience. Conscience is a voice that speaks to us from within ourselves, and it is said to be the *subjective* norm of human conduct. Conscience applies the general principles of morality expressed by the moral law or commandments to personal conduct, and it furnishes information about the rightness or wrongness of individual actions.

For example, one of the Ten Commandments obliges us to honor our parents. Let us suppose that an older son strikes his father in anger. It is conscience which tells the son that striking his father dishonored him, that his action was wrong. In other words, conscience is the application of knowledge to act.[1] It is a judgment about the rightness or wrongness of a particular action.

1 St. Thomas Aquinas, *Summa Theologiae*, Ia.79.13.

Conscience is, in a sense, an echo of the voice of God. The function of conscience is to *manifest* the correct norm of action; it does not *establish* the norm. Therefore, conscience is always dependent on the moral law; it is not a law unto itself. It follows that everyone should try to learn the will of God in his or her own regard. This process is known as the "formation of conscience." Forming one's conscience includes informing it intellectually and cultivating the virtues which are required for an upright life.

The Bible knows the reality that we call conscience even though it does not always use the word.

In the Old Testament, the Book of Genesis tells how Adam and Eve reproached themselves for having disobeyed God (Gn 3:7-11). David recognized that he had sinned grievously when he took a census of the people (2 S 24:10). In the midst of his trials, Job tells us, his heart did not rebuke him for any of his actions (Jb 27:6). The Book of Wisdom says that wickedness is accompanied by a distressed conscience (Ws 17:11).

In the New Testament, we find not only the concept of conscience, but also the word, especially in the letters of Paul. For example, Paul tells us his conscience testified that he had fulfilled his apostolate with purity of intention (2 Cor 1:12; Ac 23:1; 24:16). As the law served the Jews, so conscience served the pagans (Rm 2:15). Christians should submit to civil authorities not only to escape punishment but also for the sake of conscience (Rm 13:5). Whoever acts against his or her conscience, even when it is erroneous, commits sin (Rm 14:14, 23). Sometimes, the weak conscience of a brother may compel me to forgo the otherwise legitimate exercise of my freedom (1 Cor 8:1-10). The judgment of conscience is always subject to that of God (1 Cor 4:4). Love springs from a pure heart, a good conscience, and sincere faith (1 Tm 1:5). Some have made shipwreck of their faith by rejecting the guidance of conscience (1 Tm 1:19). Men with seared consciences have forbidden marriage and required abstinence from foods (1 Tm 4:2). The minds and consciences of defiled unbelievers, for whom nothing is clean, are tainted (Tt 1:15).

The Second Vatican Council had much to say about the role of conscience. For example, the Council said this: "In the depths of his conscience, man detects a law which he does not impose upon himself, a law which holds him to obedience. Always summoning him to love good and avoid evil, the voice of conscience can, when necessary, speak to his heart more specifically, saying: 'Do this' or 'Shun that.' For man in his heart has a law written by God. To obey it is the very dignity of man, and he will be judged according to it. Conscience is the most secret core and sanctuary of man. There he is alone with God, whose voice echoes in the depths of his being. In a wonderful manner conscience reveals that law which is fulfilled by love of God and neighbor."[2]

In its Declaration on Religious Freedom, the Second Vatican Council also clarified its mind on conscience: "Man perceives and acknowledges the imperatives of the divine law through the mediation of conscience. In all his activity a man is bound to follow his conscience faithfully, in order that he may come to God, for whom he was created. It follows that he is not to be forced to act in a manner contrary to his conscience. Nor, on the other hand, is he to be restrained from acting in accordance with his conscience, especially in matters of religion."[3]

The Second Vatican Council made this comment too: "In the formation of their consciences, the Christian faithful ought to attend carefully to the sacred and certain doctrines of the Church, for the Church is, by the will of Christ, the teacher of the truth."[4]

2 Constitution on the Church Today, no. 16.
3 Declaration on Religious Freedom, no. 3.
4 Declaration on Religious Freedom, no. 14.

Finally, a word about freedom of conscience. "Freedom of conscience" is an abstraction. Actually, a *person* is free to follow his or her own conscience. This means that an individual, in following his or her own conscience, ought to be free of coercion in any form. He or she ought to be free of unjust penalties and free to seek true personal fulfillment.

At the same time, everyone has a duty toward the true religion and toward the one Church of Christ. The duty to seek the truth and embrace it obliges the human conscience. You may ask, "Where is freedom if one has a duty?" Freedom lies in the capacity to carry out the duty in a responsible, human manner. Freedom, therefore, exists in relation to other human beings; duty exists in relation to God and the call which he gives, the demands which he makes. God calls us to serve him freely, rationally, and humanly; but he does not intend or expect us to ignore his call. His call is a true summons which makes demands on us. Acting according to one's conscience is not only a good thing, but a real obligation. The person who acts against conscience has gone astray.

In this matter of conscience there is an important difference between Catholics and some other Christians. Some Christians believe that no one can be saved without an explicit commitment to Jesus Christ. They point to the statement of Peter: "There is no salvation through anyone else [except Jesus], nor is there any other name under heaven given to the human race by which we are to be saved" (Ac 4:12). Hence, these Christians believe that Hindus and Buddhists and others who do not have an explicit knowledge of, and commitment to, Jesus Christ cannot be saved.

This is not the position of the Catholic Church. Catholics believe with all their hearts that Jesus is the Savior of the entire human race. They believe that men and women are saved only because of Christ's saving death and resurrection. Yet Catholics do not believe that men and women are excluded from salvation just because they lack an explicit commitment to

Jesus Christ. All men and women can be saved if they follow their consciences, if they do what is right insofar as it is known to them. Even in this case Jesus is their Savior even though they are ignorant of his role. In much the same way men and women are often unaware of those who do them good. God wills the salvation of all (1 Tm 2:4), and conscience is the instrument of that salvation.

However, I hasten to add that those who have an explicit knowledge of, and commitment to, Jesus Christ are in a more advantageous position, since they have the fullness of truth and easier access to the means of salvation.

In summary, I draw three conclusions from all that I have just said: *First*, a person is bound to follow his or her conscience in order to come to God. *Second*, as a consequence, no one is to be hindered by other human beings from acting in accordance with the dictates of his or her conscience. However, freedom to follow one's conscience is restricted by the rights of others and the just requirements of public order. *Third*, no one is to be forced by other human beings to act in a manner contrary to his or her conscience. These conclusions are based on the teaching of the Second Vatican Council that in the realm of conscience men and women stand alone before God.

QUESTIONS FOR REVIEW

1. What is conscience? What is its function?
2. What does the Bible teach about conscience?
3. What is freedom of conscience?
4. In what sense is conscience the instrument of salvation?

CHAPTER 30

SIN

It is about sin that I wish to speak to you now. I am especially concerned with actual sin. Actual sin is the voluntary act of an individual who transgresses the law of God and acts against the judgment of his conscience. Actual sin is to be distinguished from original sin. Original sin is the state into which all human beings are born. It is a state of alienation from God which is the result of the rebellion of our first parents. Now, however, I am concerned with actual sins, the sins we ourselves commit.

The Bible is full of references to the reality of sin. The idea of sin is found on almost every page of the Old Testament. It is commonly described in terms which are borrowed from human relationships. According to the Old Testament, sin means missing the mark, a failure to attain a goal. Sin damages the sinner (Ezk 24:6); it is a violation of the covenant and law of Yahweh, the God of Israel (Ho 8:1). The sinner hates Yahweh (Ex 20:5; Dt 5:9). Sin is folly, and the sinner is a fool (Dt 32:6; Jr 4:22).

According to the New Testament, Jesus is the conqueror of sin.

In the Gospels of Matthew, Mark, and Luke, Jesus exercises a ministry among sinners, for he has come to call sinners and not the just (Mk 2:17). Jesus recognizes that evil deeds come from the heart of an individual (Mk 7:21). The parable of the prodigal son teaches that sin is an offense against God, that pardon is possible only with the return of the sinner to God (Lk 15:17-32). We are told that Jesus was going to shed his blood on behalf of many for the forgiveness of sins (Mt 26:28).

In the Gospel and First Letter of John, the malice of sin is stated explicitly. The sinner loves the darkness rather than the light for fear that his wicked deeds will be exposed (Jn 3:19-20). Everyone who lives in sin is a slave of sin (Jn 8:34) and the slave of the devil (1 Jn 3:8-10). Sin is lawlessness (1 Jn 3:4), wrongdoing (1 Jn 5:17), the lust of the flesh, the lust of the eyes, and the pride of life (1 Jn 2:16). In these passages sin often signifies a state or a condition which is the result of a sinful act. John also recognizes the satanic power behind the sinful acts of an individual (Jn 8:44). For John, Jesus is the conqueror of sin. He is without sin himself (Jn 8:46; 1 Jn 3:5). He is the lamb who takes away the sin of the world (Jn 1:29). He is an offering for the sins of all (1 Jn 2:2; 4:10).

The writings of Paul contain a relatively full theology of sin. In several places Paul draws up lists of sins. Sinners, such as fornicators, idolaters, adulterers, sodomites, thieves, misers, drunkards, slanderers, and others will not inherit the kingdom of heaven (1 Cor 6:9-10; Gal 5:19-21). Indeed, sin is the human condition. Both Jew and Greek are under the dominion of sin; all men and women have sinned and are thus deprived of the glory of God (Rm 2:1-3:31). According to Paul, sin reigns as a power throughout the world. Sin was introduced into the world by Adam's disobedience and so entered into all men and women (Rm 5:12-19). The wages of sin is death (Rm 6:23), and the universality of death proves that all men and women are sinners (Rm 5:12). Sin so enslaves men and women that they are unable to do what is right even when they wish to do so (Rm 7:15-25).

However, Paul holds out hope. If solidarity with Adam has involved the whole human race in sin and death, a superior solidarity with Christ has brought it acquittal and life (Rm 5:15-19). Justified by faith and baptism, the Christian has put on Christ (Gal 3:27-28). If anyone is in Christ, he is a new creation (2 Cor 5:17). He is no longer in the flesh, but in the spirit (Rm 8:9).

It is against this Biblical background that we must analyze the nature of sin. Actual sin is, as I have said, the voluntary act of an individual who transgresses the laws of God and acts against the judgment of his or her conscience. The element which renders an act sinful is turning one's back on God. Sin is a rebellion against God. It means choosing a particular object in opposition to the law of God. For example, the adulterer says in his heart: "I know God forbids me to approach another man's wife, but I will approach this man's wife despite God's law." A sinful human being wishes to be independent of God — to decide for himself or herself what is good and what is evil.

This brings me to the distinction between mortal and venial sin. All sins are not equal in gravity. Surely killing an innocent person is much more serious than an unkind remark about a neighbor. Mortal sin is a grievous offense against the law of God. It destroys one's friendship with God and the life of grace. Mortal sin is spiritual death, and it is punished with eternal damnation in hell. Venial sin, on the other hand, is a less serious offense against the law of God. It does not destroy one's friendship with God or the life of grace, but it incurs temporal punishment. When one sins mortally, the sinner turns away from God; God is no longer the goal of his or her life. There is a radical opposition between the mortally sinful act and the love of God. When one sins venially, he or she does not turn away from God; God remains the goal of life; but he or she takes a kind of detour on the road to God.

According to Catholic theologians, three conditions must be verified before one is guilty of mortal sin: 1) The matter must be grave. There must be a situation in which one's fundamental loyalty to God is at stake. The gravity of the matter can be recognized from Holy Scripture, the teaching of the Church, and common sense. All three sources tell us, for example, that killing an innocent person and adultery are gravely wrong. 2) There must be sufficient reflection on the part of the intellect, that is to say, the agent must be clearly aware of the gravely evil action he or she is contemplating. And 3) there must be full consent of the will to the gravely evil action. If any one of these conditions is not verified, then the action is not mortally sinful. It may not be a sin at all.

What are the causes of sin? Actually there is only one cause of sin, the disorderly will of the sinner. Human failure is responsible for the disorder of a sinful act. However, human beings are subject to temptation from without and within. Temptation to sin comes from the world, the flesh, and the devil. The world can tempt us to sin. Here I am thinking about those persons, places, and things which can lead us into sin. We are bound to avoid the proximate occasions of sin, those which constitute a grave danger of sinning. Some temptations arise from the flesh, from within ourselves. They arise from the disorderly and selfish drives we all experience within ourselves. Finally, some temptations come from the devil, especially if they are sudden, violent, and protracted.

Sometimes people feel no hope of resisting a particular temptation to sin. They should remember, however, that God permits no one to be tempted beyond his or her strength to resist. An excellent means of avoiding temptation is to avoid entirely those persons, places, and things that lead us into sin. The regular use of confession, the sacrament of reconciliation, is also a great help.

God does not tempt us to sin, but he permits us to be tempted. Why? Because temptations are not meant for our ruin, but for our good. They are meant to strengthen the nerve and sinew of our minds and hearts and souls. How does a football player increase his strength? By lifting weights and scrimmaging with other players. How does a sprinter increase her speed? By competing with other sprinters. That is what temptation is meant to do. It is the test which enables us to emerge the stronger for the fight.

My good friends, let us flee sin at all costs. It is the only real evil, the only thing that can separate us from God.

QUESTIONS FOR REVIEW

1. What is actual sin?
2. What does the Bible teach about sin?
3. What is the difference between mortal and venial sin?
4. What conditions must be verified before one is guilty of a mortal sin?
5. What is the cause of sin?
6. Whence comes temptation to sin?
7. How can we resist temptation?
8. Why does God permit us to be tempted?

CHAPTER 31

FAITH

My subject for this occasion is the subject of faith or belief. Having spoken about the moral law and conscience in general, I must now discuss in particular those actions commanded or forbidden by the moral law and conscience. The first of these actions is faith to which doubt and disbelief are opposed. Faith is of fundamental importance for the Christian life, for it is impossible to lead a Christian life without it.

The New Testament has a great deal to say about faith, but in each instance we must examine the context closely in order to get at the meaning. In the Gospels of Matthew, Mark, and Luke, Jesus himself demands faith (Mt 9:28-29; Mk 4:40), praises faith (Mt 8:10; Lk 7:9), and declares that faith has saved a person from an illness which is miraculously cured (Mt 9:22; Mk 5:34; Lk 8:48). For one who believes, Jesus said, all things are possible (Mk 9:23-24), and even a small amount of faith can move mountains (Mt 17:20; 21:21). In these Gospels faith means basically the acceptance of Jesus and his claims.

When I read the words of Jesus about the power of faith to move mountains, I think of the old man who lived in the shadow of a mountain. His house was cold and dark, so he decided to get rid of the mountain by faith. One night, as he got ready for bed, he tried to muster as much faith as he could. Then he slept. The next morning he looked out the window, and the mountain was still there. "You stubborn old mountain," he said to himself, "I knew you'd be there."

There is a much fuller treatment of faith in the letters of Paul. For Paul, faith in Christ Jesus makes a person righteous or acceptable to God (Rm 3:22, 26, 28, 30; Gal 2:16; 3:8, 24). Through faith Christians become children of God in Christ Jesus (Gal 3:26). By grace we have been saved through faith; salvation is a gift of God; it is not from our works (Ep 2:8-9). Faith comes about through hearing the word of God (Rm 10:13-15). One's faith must be externalized (Rm 10:9-10) and give rise to deeds of love (Gal 5:6).

For Paul, then, faith means acceptance of Christ. This acceptance of Christ is not merely an intellectual acceptance of a body of truth (although faith does include an intellectual element), but it is also a surrender and total commitment to the person of the Savior. This commitment is not made by a single act. Christians may at times suffer shortcomings in their faith (1 Th 3:10). And they ought to grow in faith (2 Cor 10:15) to the extent that the believer lives with Christ, crucified with him (Gal 2:19-20).

In the Letter to the Hebrews we find a lengthy discussion of faith which goes its own way. Faith is defined as "the realization of what is hoped for and evidence of things not seen" (Heb 11:1). The author goes on to cite many examples of holy men in the Old Testament who displayed such faith. In the Letter of James we also find an important reference to faith. There James concludes that faith without works is as dead as a body without breath (Jm 2:14-26).

We see, therefore, that there are two elements which go to make up New Testament faith: *first*, an intellectual element which accepts the truth of God revealed through Jesus Christ, and *second*, a volitional element which surrenders oneself to God through Jesus Christ. Both elements are essential: one cannot surrender himself or herself without first accepting the truth of God's revelation; but this acceptance is of no avail unless surrender and commitment follow.

Let us consider first the intellectual element of faith. I shall say more about surrender and commitment when I speak about hope and love.

The official teachers of the Catholic Church, especially the bishops of the First and Second Vatican Councils, have analyzed the intellectual element of New Testament faith very closely. According to the First Vatican Council (1869-70), faith is an assent of the intellect, under the influence of grace, to a truth revealed by God, not because we understand it, but because God, who can neither deceive nor be deceived, has revealed it.[1] Thus, Catholics accept the mystery of the three distinct persons in the one God on faith; that is to say, they accept it not because they understand it, but because God has revealed it. What God has revealed has been made known to us especially through his divine Son, Jesus Christ, who has been accredited to us by his miraculous deeds and his resurrection from the dead. We see, therefore, that faith, as I have described it, is a rational service, completely worthy of a thinking person. The bishops of the Second Vatican Council (1962-65) concurred in this analysis.[2]

We often take the word of another for something we do not understand. I have used this example before: when we see a stone lying on the ground, it appears perfectly inactive. Yet, physicists tell us that in reality the stone is a beehive of activity, for, they say, the smallest particles of that stone, its atoms and molecules, are quite active. How there can be activity in a stone is a mystery to us; still, we are willing to believe what the physicists tell us, because we regard them as knowledgeable individuals.

1 Cf. J. Neuner, S.J., and J. Dupuis, S.J., *The Christian Faith* (Staten Island: Alba House, 1982), p. 42, no. 118.

2 Constitution on Divine Revelation, nos. 5-6; Declaration on Religious Freedom, no. 10.

It's much the same with respect to the mysteries of the Christian faith, whether we are speaking of the Holy Trinity, the Incarnation of God's Son, the life of grace, or some other mystery. We accept all these things as true because God had revealed them through Jesus. We know that God is knowledge and truth; consequently, we take on faith whatever he tells us, whether we understand it or not.

Faith, understood as an assent to truth, resides in the intellect of human beings. But the will also concurs in the act of believing because the truths to which the intellect assents lack the evidence which usually determines the assent of the intellect. The intervention of the will is necessary to move the intellect to adhere to the revealed truth. In this way the act of faith is of its very nature a free act. Because faith rests on the authority of God revealing and not on the intrinsic evidence of truth, it is obscure; but it is nonetheless firm and certain. Furthermore, both in its beginning and its development, faith is always the effect of God's grace.

Catholics often speak of the "deposit of faith," by which they mean the "stock" or "treasure" of truths revealed by God to his people. These are contained in the tradition of the Church (its life, worship, preaching, and practice) and the Bible. It is the responsibility of the official teachers of the Church, the Pope and the bishops, to preserve the deposit of faith with its revealed truths and to expound it faithfully for the benefit of all. Their task is to make the deposit of faith comprehensible, credible, and fruitful in a constantly evolving world.

Every disciple of Christ has the obligation of spreading the faith as time and circumstances permit. Bishops are the preachers of the faith above all others. They preach the faith Catholics must believe and put into practice. Bishops share the responsibility to preach with their priests. Lay Catholics spread the faith by living the faith in those situations accessible to them alone and by saying an appropriate word to those who are receptive. Missionaries carry the faith to those who have never heard it. The Church must also employ the modern media of communication to spread the faith. These reach into almost every place.

QUESTIONS FOR REVIEW

1. What does the New Testament say about faith?
2. What are the two elements of New Testament faith?
3. Why do Catholics take on faith truths they do not understand?
4. Why is faith worthy of a thinking person?
5. If faith is obscure, how can it be firm and certain?
6. How does faith involve the intellect? The will?
7. What is the deposit of faith?
8. Who is obliged to spread the faith?

CHAPTER 32

HOPE AND LOVE

On the last occasion I spoke about the intellectual element of faith, and now I wish to say more about surrender and commitment by speaking of hope and love. It seems to me that hope and love are largely equivalent to the surrender and commitment of New Testament faith.

The Old Testament breathes an atmosphere of hope. Yahweh, the God of Israel, was the hope of Israel (Jr 14:8; 17:13). The reason for hope was that Yahweh was faithful to his promises (Dt 32:4; Nb 23:19), and his mighty deeds in the past testified to his power to help (Gn 15:7; Ex 6:6). The object of the hope of the patriarchs was that of descendants in great numbers and the possession of the land promised to them (Gn 17:8; Ex 3:8). The destruction of the kingdom of Israel in 721 B.C. and of the kingdom of Judah in 587 B.C. dealt a severe blow to the hopes of God's people. However, the prophets enkindled those hopes in a different way. Jeremiah spoke of a new covenant which God would write upon the hearts of his people (Jr 31:31; 32:38-41). Ezekiel promised that God would remember his covenant with Israel, giving his people a new heart and a new spirit (Ezk 36:25-28). Still, the hope of Israel fell short of the grave, since the Old Testament had no idea of true life after death until its latest books.

In the New Testament, the doctrine of hope is developed especially in the Pauline writings. As we read in Paul's Letter to the Romans, Abraham is the model of hope for he was "hoping against hope" (Rm 4:18). The Christian is saved through hope whose object is not seen (Rm 8:24). Hope is the fruit of proved virtue and endurance (Rm 5:4). There are three things that remain: faith, hope, and love (1 Cor 13:13). The object of hope is resurrection (1 Cor 15:19). Hope distinguishes the Christian from the Gentiles who are without hope, especially for life after death (Ep 2:12). According to the author of the Letter to the Hebrews, hope is a firm anchor which extends beyond the veil (Heb 6:19). In the Bible, I must note, every promise of reward is an implied commandment to hope.

The Catholic Church has developed its teaching about hope against this Scriptural background. For the Catholic, hope is the virtue by which we firmly trust that God, who is merciful and all-powerful, will give us eternal happiness and the means to attain it. In other words, the object of our hope is eternal happiness with God in heaven and the means to attain it. The Christian virtue of hope is rooted in the mercy and power of God. We could not hope for salvation if God were not merciful, for without God's good will we would be left unaided. More important still is the power of God. If God wanted to save us but were unable to do so, we would always run the risk of being lost. Since, however, God is almighty, he is able to help us achieve the object of our hope. Thus, the firmness of our hope is frequently represented in art by an anchor. Seen in this light, hope means surrender and commitment to God through Jesus Christ, upon whom we rely for our salvation.

Yet, solid though our anchor of hope may be, we must still work out our salvation in fear and trembling in view of human willfulness. We must not neglect to pray for ourselves nor to seek the fonts of divine grace. To despair of salvation as well as to presume to gain it without personal effort is to sin against hope. Both as a virtue and as an act, hope resides in the human will. As faith gives way to vision in the afterlife, so hope gives way to possession.

If the Old Testament breathes an atmosphere of hope, it is permeated with love too. The idea of love is especially prominent in the Book of Deuteronomy. There the selection of the Israelites as the people of God is seen as a matter of free choice and love on the part of God (Dt 7:6-8). Out of love the Lord led the Israelites out of Egypt (Dt 4:37; 7:8). The Lord promised to love and bless and multiply them (Dt 7:13). In turn the Israelites were commanded to love the Lord their God with all their heart, with all their soul, and with all their strength (Dt 6:5). The Israelites were to love the Lord and heed his statutes, decrees, and commandments (Dt 11:1). Other passages in the Old Testament, such as those in Daniel and Nehemiah (Dn 9:4; Ne 1:15), for example, speak of the connection between love and the observance of God's commandments.

In the New Testament, Jesus identified the great commandment of the law as love of God and neighbor (Mt 22:34-40). One's neighbor is even a person from whom one is alienated (Lk 10:29-37). Jesus commanded us to love even our enemies (Mt 5:43-48). He taught that love of God must be exclusive, suffering no rival (Mt 6:24; Lk 16:13), that our love for himself must be greater than our love for parents or children (Mt 10:37).

The Apostle Paul had much to say about Christian love. The love of God has been poured out into our hearts through the Holy Spirit (Rm 5:5). God has proved his love for us in that Christ died for us while we were still sinners (Rm 5:8). No trial or creature can separate us from the love of God in Christ Jesus (Rm 8:35-39). All things work together for the good for those who love God (Rm 8:28). Love builds the Christian community (1 Cor 8:1). Love is the way which surpasses all others; it is the most excellent of all the gifts which are of no value without it; and it remains even after faith and hope disappear (1 Cor 13:1-13). Husbands should love their wives as Christ loves the

Church (Ep 5:25). Love is the root and foundation of the Christian life (Ep 3:17).

Love is a prominent theme in the Johannine writings, too. Jesus loved his own to the very end (Jn 13:1). Love for Jesus is shown by keeping his commandments (Jn 14:15, 21, 23). The new commandment of Jesus is to love one another (Jn 13:34; 15:17). As the Father loved Jesus, so Jesus loved the disciples (Jn 15:9). The Father and Son abide with one who loves Jesus (Jn 14:23). As Jesus laid down his life for us, so we ought to lay down our lives for our brothers (1 Jn 3:16). The one who is without love knows nothing of God, for God is love (1 Jn 4:8, 16). Through love for one another we can be certain that God dwells in us and brings his love to perfection (1 Jn 4:7-21). These are just a few of the thoughts about love taken from the writings of John and his circle.

The Catholic Church has developed its teaching about love against this Scriptural background. The word, love, is used so frequently these days. People say they love their children, their dog, or football. For Christians, however, love is the supreme virtue. By it we place God before all other persons and things, and regard our neighbor as ourselves for love of God. Love is the fulfillment of the great commandment of the Christian religion. Love means dedication to God and neighbor and a well-ordered concern for ourselves. To love God is to make God the center of our lives and to keep his commandments. To love one's neighbor is to treat him or her with invincible good will. Love is the spirit which should prevail between husbands and wives, between parents and children, and indeed among all men and women despite their race and creed.

From all this we understand that love is not a matter of feeling. It resides in the human will. It is a supernatural gift of God, and it can grow in intensity. Love is lost by serious sin, but it can be recovered by repentance. Love remains even in the afterlife when we shall be with our Father in heaven. Love includes even our enemies. It means that we always seek their true good, punishing them perhaps for wrong-doing, but with a view to their improvement. True love for self obliges us to employ the ordinary means to preserve life and health. Love impels us to assist a brother or sister in need; thus, the duty of fraternal correction and giving to the poor. Love forbids us to lead others into sin or to cooperate in their sins.

My dear friends, our divine Savior himself gave us the supreme example of love. He came down from heaven not to do his own will but the will of the One who sent him. (Jn 6:38). He came to serve rather than to be served (Mt 20:28). The supreme task of our lives is to follow his noble example.

QUESTIONS FOR REVIEW

1. What is Christian hope?
2. What does the Bible say about hope?
3. Does hope exclude all fear and trembling from the Christian life?
4. What is Christian love?
5. What does the Bible say about love?
6. What are the implications of love?

CHAPTER 33

Worship (I)
RITES AND OBSERVANCES

Not only must we believe in, hope in, and love God above all things, but we must also worship him. By this I mean that we must pay God the respect and honor due him as the Supreme Being. Our worship of God is of no particular benefit to him. We are the beneficiaries when we worship God. It is about worship that I wish to speak to you on this occasion.

In the Old Testament there are many references to worship. The sole object of worship was Yahweh, the God of Israel, who could not be represented by any image (Ex 20:2-5; Dt 5:2-10). Worship of other gods, sorcery, magic, divination, human sacrifice, and worship of the dead were all condemned. Worship itself was characterized by such cultural institutions as the ark of the covenant, a priesthood, various kinds of sacrifices, and a calendar of annual religious feasts. However, the worship commanded by God was rooted in the right inward disposition, especially the love of God. The prophets stressed the futility of ritual worship that lacked the proper interior disposition. For example, we read in the Book of Isaiah:

> "What care I for the number of your sacrifices? says the Lord.
> I have had enough of whole-burnt rams and the fat of fatlings;

In the blood of calves, lambs, and goats I find no pleasure. . .
Wash yourselves clean!
Put away misdeeds from before my eyes;
cease doing evil; learn to do good.
Make justice your aim; redress the wronged;
hear the orphan's plea; defend the widow"
(Is 1:11, 16-17).

In the New Testament Jesus and his disciples practiced the traditional forms of Jewish worship. For example, Jesus was accustomed to eat the Passover supper with his disciples. Jesus quoted with approval the injunction of Deuteronomy: "The Lord, your God, shall you worship, and him alone shall you serve" (Mt 4:10). Jesus himself prayed to God both publicly and privately, and he taught his disciples the prayer known as the Lord's Prayer (Mt 6:9-13). Following the prophetic tradition, Jesus taught that we authentically worship the Father in Spirit and truth (Jn 4:23). If worship is to be real, we must be at peace with our brothers and sisters: "If you bring your gift to the altar," Jesus taught in his Sermon on the Mount, "and there recall that your brother has anything against you, leave your gift there at the altar, go first and be reconciled with your brother, and then come and offer your gift" (Mt 5:23-24).

After Pentecost, the apostles continued to observe the Jewish ritual. For example, they continued to pray in the temple (Ac 3:1), but at the same time they began to honor Jesus as Lord and Messiah (Ac 2:36). The reenactment of the Last Supper was the center of the new worship (Mk 14:22-24; 1 Cor 11:17-34). The "breaking of the bread" was held on the first day of the week instead of the sabbath (Ac 2:42; 1 Cor 16:2) to commemorate the resurrection. Besides the Eucharist, other Christian ordinances, such as baptism, anointing of the sick, and the imposition of hands, were employed (Ac 8:38; Jm 5:14; Ac 6:6; 8:17).

Catholics employ many forms of worship. I think, first of all, of the sacraments: baptism, confirmation, Holy Eucharist, penance or the sacrament of reconciliation, anointing of the sick, holy orders and matrimony. It is the belief of Catholics that these sacraments go back to the words and deeds of Christ. The purpose of the sacraments is to restore and intensify the friendship between God and his sons and daughters, to build up the body of Christ, the Church, and to give worship to God. It is the conviction of Catholics that each sacrament is an act of Christ worshipping his heavenly Father. For example, Paul teaches that it is Christ who baptizes when the human minister baptizes (Ep 5:26). Needless to say, however, if the sacraments are to be fruitful acts of worship on our part, we must receive them with the proper dispositions. These include faith, repentance, and commitment to God and his Son Jesus Christ.

Related to the sacraments which were instituted by Christ are the sacramentals which were instituted by the Church. Just as Christ employed material things such as water, oil, bread and wine for the sacraments, so the Church employs material things for the sacramentals. The sacramentals are material objects blessed by the Church. For example, the Church has composed blessings for food, musical instruments, bells, fire engines, automobiles, and many other things. In blessing these objects the Church prays that those who use these things may have divine favor and be more closely consecrated to divine worship. Sacramentals are part of the Church's mission to sanctify all things: the material order, time and space, and the human beings for whom these things exist.

An important part of Catholic worship is the observance of Sunday. In the Book of Revelation Sunday is called the Lord's day (Rv 1:10). From the earliest times Christians have been accustomed to hear the word of God and celebrate the Lord's Supper on Sundays, for it was on Sunday that Jesus rose from the dead. The heart of Sunday worship for Catholics is the Mass. The first part of the Mass consists largely of readings from Sacred Scripture together with a homily by the priest. The purpose of the homily is to explain the significance of the Scriptural readings for the present moment. The second part of the Mass is the celebration of the Lord's Supper which Our Lord enjoined us to do in memory of him.

The worship of the Catholic Church has undergone certain revisions in recent years in order to foster the fullest participation of the faithful in the services. One of the reasons for substituting the vernacular in place of Latin was to afford everyone a better opportunity to understand and to participate in the worship of the Church. The law of the Church imposes a serious obligation upon all the faithful to attend Mass every Sunday and holy day of obligation (c. 1247). This law is understandable in the light of our natural duty to worship God and the place of the Mass in Catholic tradition.

Sunday is also a day of rest in the Catholic tradition. It continues the long tradition of the sabbath rest in the Old Testament. Sunday should be a day of joy and freedom from work. The Sunday rest should provide an unhurried time for reflection and the development of one's interior life. It should provide a break from the routine of the work-a-day world to allow the cultivation of higher values including the strengthening of family and community ties. It is not always easy to say what work should be avoided on Sunday. Both the changing American culture as well as the needs of the individual are important factors that need to be considered. In general, we should abstain from those works and activities which are incompatible with Sunday worship and personal renewal.

Finally, I must say a word about the liturgical year. Civil society has its calendar marked with public holidays and observances such as Memorial Day and the Fourth of July. The Church too has its calendar marked with its recollection and celebration of the great events in the life of Christ. In this way Catholics join themselves in spirit with their Lord and Savior. The Church's year revolves around the two great celebrations of Easter and Christmas. However, the Church's calendar also includes the memory of Mary, the Mother of God, and the memory of the saints who followed so closely in the footsteps of Jesus and provided a marvelous example of the Christian life.

QUESTIONS FOR REVIEW

1. What is worship?
2. What does the Bible say about the worship of God?
3. What are some of the forms of worship employed by Catholics?
4. How are the sacramentals like the sacraments? How are they unlike?
5. What is the importance of Sunday for the Catholic?
6. What is the liturgical year?

CHAPTER 34

Worship (II)
SINGING AND PRAYER

In this talk I should like to say something about singing and private prayer. These, too, are forms of worship.

It is important that the members of a congregation take an active part in the worship services of the Church. Through active participation they derive greater benefit from the services. It's something like exercise. We derive more benefit from exercising ourselves than from watching others exercise. Singing is one form of active participation in the worship of the Church. Singing is one way by which a congregation expresses its sentiments of worship. It is difficult for one who feels strongly to remain silent, for "song befits the lover,"[1] as St. Augustine (354-410) said long ago; and, as the ancient saying has it, "one who sings well prays twice." Thus the Church on earth joins its song to the song of the Church in heaven, and together they sing a wondrous hymn of praise to the Holy Trinity.

Congregational singing not only expresses one's sentiments of worship, but it also arouses the faith and piety of large gatherings of people. It's something like the singing of the national anthem before a sporting event. Who does not experience a surge of patriotism while the crowd is singing the "Star-Spangled Banner"? Much the same thing happens when

1 Sermon 336, no. 1.

the congregation joins in the singing of a hymn. There is a new dedication, a new stirring of faith, a rekindling of hope when a hymn is sung. The singing of a congregation rises to heaven like the bursting of a thunderous sea,[2] as St. Ambrose (340-397) wrote long ago. By the melody of their song Catholics testify to the unity of their hearts and minds, a unity that is fitting for children of the same Father.

The New Testament praises sacred song. Paul wrote to the Christians of ancient Ephesus: "Be filled with the Spirit, addressing one another [in] psalms and hymns and spiritual songs, singing and playing to the Lord in your hearts" (Ep 5:18-19). And in his Letter to the Colossians, Paul wrote: "Let the word of Christ dwell in you richly, as in all wisdom you teach and admonish one another, singing psalms, hymns, and spiritual songs with gratitude in your hearts to God" (Col 3:16). It is difficult to exaggerate the importance of singing as an element of Catholic worship.

Then there is the worship of private prayer. By private prayer I mean praying as individuals and raising our minds and hearts to God, fixing our attention on him and expressing our love for him. Our Lord himself commended private prayer by word and example. "When you pray," he said in his Sermon on the Mount, "go to your inner room, close the door, and pray to your Father in secret. And your Father, who sees in secret, will repay you" (Mt 6:6). In Luke's Gospel we read that Jesus followed his own recommendation and spent a whole night on the mountain in communion with God. This prayer was the prelude to his choice of the twelve apostles (Lk 6:12-16). One of the most precious accounts of the prayer of Jesus is the Gethsemane episode, in which Jesus revealed his inner conflict prior to his passion and death (Mt 26:36-46). The seventeenth chapter of John's Gospel records the long prayer of Jesus for his disciples and all believers. Every rabbi taught his

2 Cf. *Hexameron* 3, 5, 23.

disciples a short prayer that they might use regularly, and Jesus taught his disciples the short prayer that we know as the Lord's Prayer or the Our Father (Mt 6:9-13).

When we pray, Jesus said, we should pray with the confidence of sons and daughters who approach their Father with a request (Mt 7:7-11; Lk 11:9-13). We should pray with the importunity of a person who petitions a neighbor for bread until the neighbor yields in order to get rid of him (Lk 11:5-8). Christians are to pray always and not lose heart (Lk 18:1-8). True, we do not always receive precisely what we ask for in prayer, but we always receive something good in response to prayer. For example, Paul asked the Lord three times to be delivered from a "thorn in the flesh," possibly the attack of enemies. Instead, he received the strength to bear the situation (2 Cor 12:7-9). Whatever we ask the Father in Jesus' name will be given to us (Jn 15:16). Jesus lives to make intercession for us (Heb 7:25). Through Jesus we have acquired a spirit of adoption by which we cry out to the Father (Rm 8:15).

It is true that God does not always give us exactly what we ask for in prayer. But there is a reason for that. Let me give you an example. When I was in the sixth grade, I had a friend named Billy. His father had a collection of rifles which were chained to the wall, and I used to admire them when I visited Billy's home. Billy also owned a small calibre rifle. I wished I had a rifle. So I asked my father for one. He thought about it, but finally he said No. I didn't need a rifle, and it might be dangerous in my hands. Later, however, he gave me a new baseball glove for my birthday. I needed that. My old baseball glove had worn out. Sometimes that's how God answers our prayers.

God does not always give us exactly what we ask for in prayer because it may not be good for us. However, our heavenly Father always gives us something good when we pray. There is no such thing as an unanswered prayer. The question is: Are we clever enough to recognize God's answer when it comes? Paul asked to be delivered from his thorn in the flesh; instead, he received the strength to bear it.

There are many who believe that prayer is something useless. They say, for example, that it is nothing more than a device, invented by someone, to relieve the sense of futility that we experience in a situation with which we cannot cope. Others say that Almighty God knows our needs, so that we do not have to tell him what they are. Others say that what we seem to obtain by prayer is only the result of our own efforts or the happy coincidence of circumstances beyond our control. Still others reject prayer because our requests are slow to be answered or do not seem to be answered at all.

For the Christian, all these objections to prayer miss the mark. Our Lord Jesus Christ recommended that we pray. He taught his disciples to pray. He promised an answer to those who pray. For the Christian, this recommendation of prayer by the Son of God himself is sufficient to establish the value of prayer beyond all shadow of doubt.

We pray, not that we may change God, but that we may seek that which God had disposed to be fulfilled by our prayers. We pray, not that we may inform God of our needs, but that we may look to God as the source of all good and our refuge in time of difficulty. It is true that we cannot always distinguish what is the result of prayer and what is the result of natural means. For example, we cannot always tell to what extent recovery from sickness is the result of the doctor's pills or the result of prayer. No matter! God is at work in either case. It is true that we do not always obtain what we ask for in prayer; but we have seen that there is no such thing as an unanswered prayer.

Catholics recognize many forms of private prayer such as morning and evening prayers, prayers at meal time, the rosary, the way of the cross, devotions to the saints, meditation, and spontaneous prayer shared by the members of a family or a small group. Each one will fasten upon that form of private prayer most helpful to him or her. It is well to have a fixed time for prayer — to decide, for example, that I am going to say the rosary daily just before I go to bed. In this way prayer is more apt to become a part of one's life.

Unquestionably, it is not easy to pray. The frantic world in which we live is not conducive to prayer. Still, the decision to pray or not to pray rests ultimately with ourselves. The rewards of private prayer are enormous: communion with God our Father who is Lord of heaven and earth, greater docility to the inspirations of the Holy Spirit, a heightened awareness of one's brothers and sisters, the satisfactions of spiritual and material needs, refreshment for our weary spirits, and progress on the road to eternal life.

QUESTIONS FOR REVIEW

1. What is the reason for singing in Catholic worship?
2. What does the New Testament say about sacred song?
3. What is meant by private prayer?
4. What did Jesus think of private prayer?
5. Does God always answer our prayers?
6. What are the various forms of private prayer?
7. What are the rewards of private prayer?

CHAPTER 35

TRUTH, FIDELITY, AND HONOR

On this occasion, I wish to speak to you about some other actions by which we seek God. These actions are telling the truth, fidelity to one's promises, and honoring those who merit it.

Truth, fidelity, and honor have to do with those interior values which enable people to live in peace and harmony with each other. To tell the truth is to say what a person believes to be factual. A witness tells the truth when she describes an automobile accident exactly as she remembers it. Telling the truth is necessary if there is to be trust among people. Fidelity is allied to truthfulness. The faithful person sticks to his or her convictions and promises. To honor someone is to give that person the respect or deference due to him or her because of his or her position in the community or because of intrinsic merit. For example, the mayor of a city deserves to be honored because of his position in the community. An old person is entitled to respect simply because of the wisdom that comes with the passing years.

The word, truth, is used in the Bible with several meanings; but here I am interested in Biblical truth insofar as it signifies the conformity of what is said to the facts. The Old Testament condemns the lie in several passages. For example, the eighth of the Ten Commandments forbids us to bear false witness against a neighbor (Ex 20:16), and the prophet

Jeremiah condemns those whose mouth utters deceit (Jr 9:7). Yet, in some passages, the Old Testament seems to condone falsehood for a good purpose, as in the case of Abraham who told the Egyptians that Sarai was his sister, while in reality she was his wife (Gn 12:11 ff).

The New Testament is more strict in rejecting lying. In his Sermon on the Mount, Jesus taught that the Yes and No of his disciples should be so reliable that they do not need to take an oath (Mt 5:37). In the Gospel of John the devil is characterized as the father of lies (Jn 8:44). The Apostle Paul wrote to the Ephesians: "Putting away falsehood, speak the truth, each one to his neighbor, for we are members of one another" (Ep 4:25). Needless to say, telling the truth is necessary for the good of society; and it is a sin to tell a lie.

Connected with telling the truth is telling the truth under oath. An oath means calling upon God to witness the truth of what we say. Usually a witness is called upon to take an oath in a court of law. In the Old Testament the Israelites were commanded to swear only by calling upon the name of the Lord (Dt 6:13), and they were forbidden to swear falsely (Lv 19:12). In the New Testament Jesus seems to forbid oaths. He said in his Sermon on the Mount: "Do not swear at all. . . . Let your 'Yes' mean 'Yes' and your 'No' mean 'No' " (Mt 5:34-37). Quite generally, Biblical scholars, who understand the Jewish manner of speaking in the New Testament, tell us that these words of Jesus about oaths are not to be taken literally.

In effect Jesus is saying that in the ordinary conduct of human affairs we should be so trustworthy that we don't have to invoke the divine name to testify to the truth. The Apostle Paul often took an oath, calling upon God to witness to the truth of what he said (e.g., Gal 1:20). Catholics regard perjury, that is to say, lying under oath, as a mortal sin.

Up to this point I have been speaking about truthfulness. Then there is the matter of fidelity to one's promises and commitments. This is necessary for the good of society. Take a very simple example. Suppose that I promise to take a sick person to the doctor in my automobile. If I fail to keep my promise, then both the sick person and the doctor are inconvenienced, to say the least. A failure to keep one's promise which results in grave harm to another is a serious sin.

A vow is a promise made to God. For example, the members of Catholic religious orders, such as the Franciscans or the Sisters of Mercy, make a vow of chastity. They vow to remain unmarried and to refrain from those actions which are permissible to married people alone. They make this vow so that they can devote themselves freely to God's work without the responsibility of a family. To make a vow strengthens one's resolve to fulfill the good work promised to God. To violate a vow of this nature is a serious sin. A vow should never be made without sufficient reflection and the advice of a prudent Christian. In making a vow a person should avoid haste and levity and should seriously consider the responsibility to be assumed.

Fidelity also means faithfulness to one's commitments. For example, two young people make a commitment to each other when they get married. If their marriage is to be valid, if it is to be a true marriage, they make a life-long commitment to each other. It is not love but the mutual commitment of husband and wife to each other that makes a marriage. The law of Christ and the good of society require that husband and wife be faithful to this commitment. Without commitment few important tasks can be accomplished, whether it be a marriage, gaining an education, or writing a book. Commitment and perseverance pay off.

Finally, there is the matter of honor. Honor means the esteem we have for others and the respect we show them. Others merit our esteem and respect because of their personal worth or place in the community. The Scriptures speak of the duty to honor others. For example, one of the Ten Commandments obliges us to honor our parents (Ex 20:12). In his

Sermon on the Mount Jesus rebukes those who use abusive language toward their brothers and sisters and hold them in contempt (Mt 5:22). The Apostle Paul encourages the Romans to give respect and honor to everyone who deserves them, and to anticipate one another in showing respect (Rm13:7). James forbids discrimination between rich and poor in the Christian assembly, for to do so is to dishonor the poor whom God chose to be the heirs of the kingdom (Jm 2:2-6).

Of course, God merits the highest honor and respect. Then those persons who more than others reflect the nature of God merit our honor and respect. These are the Mother of God and the saints. Children owe honor and respect to their parents who stand in the place of God. The citizens of the country owe honor and respect to the President and other civil officials because of their position. Those who develop their God-given talents merit honor and respect for what they have achieved. Ultimately, every person merits honor and respect because each one is made in the image of God. This honor is due a person regardless of moral achievements or failure.

One is guilty of contumely by dishonoring another person. We can dishonor another person in several ways — by speaking to him or treating her rudely, by mocking his representative, or by disfiguring her picture or image. The evil consists in depriving the person of the honor which is due him or her. The words of Jesus are very strong: "Any man who uses abusive language towards his brother shall be answerable to the Sanhedrin, and if he holds him in contempt he risks the fires of Gehenna" (Mt 5:22).

We can dishonor another by detraction, that is to say, by revealing the secret fault of another without sufficient reason. Everyone has a right to his good name. However, this right to a good name is conditioned by the good of society. Sometimes secret faults have to be revealed. For example, a person seeking an important public office is scrutinized to see if he or she is a worthy candidate; and relevant hidden faults ought to be revealed.

We can dishonor another person by calumny or slander, that is to say, by deliberately intending to blacken another's reputation through misrepresentation. Calumny has the added malice of a lie. The Scriptures speak very harshly of calumny or slander. One can cooperate in the defamation of another merely by listening to the defamer. To elicit detraction or slander is the moral equivalent of speaking it.

My good friends, I have been speaking to you about telling the truth, being faithful to one's promises, and honoring others. These things are approved by God and common sense.

QUESTIONS FOR REVIEW

1. What does it mean to tell the truth?
2. What does the Bible say about lying?
3. What is an oath?
4. What did Jesus say about oaths?
5. What is fidelity?
6. What is a vow?
7. How do we honor another person?
8. Who merits honor?
9. How can we dishonor another person?

CHAPTER 36

Justice (I)
THE BASIS OF JUSTICE

On this occasion, I should like to take up the matter of justice. By acting justly we draw closer to God.

The words, justice and just, are found in the Bible. Generally, they have a very comprehensive meaning signifying righteousness in the sight of God. In this sense, the just person is one who is obedient to God in all things and acts in complete accord with the divine law. For example, the Book of Genesis uses the word, just, to describe a person who keeps the way of the Lord (Gn 18:19) and is upright and blameless in all things (Gn 18:23-32). The prophet Malachi makes a distinction between the just and the wicked, that is to say, between him who serves God and him who does not serve him (Ml 3:18).

We find the words, justice and just, used in the same comprehensive sense in the New Testament. For instance, Jesus tells us in the Sermon on the Mount to love even our enemies: "I say to you, love your enemies, and pray for those who persecute you, that you may be children of your heavenly Father, for he makes his sun to rise on the bad and the good, and causes rain to fall on the just and the unjust" (Mt 5:44-45). Jesus advises us to seek first the kingdom of God and his justice, and all else that we need will be given us besides (Mt 6:33). If we are to enter the kingdom of God, our justice must exceed that of the scribes and Pharisees (Mt 5:20).

Paul continues this usage in his letters. He too understands the words, justice and just, in a comprehensive sense to mean acceptance by God and obedience to the divine will. As he writes in his Letter to the Romans, justice or righteousness comes not by observing the Mosaic Law, but by faith in Jesus (Rm 3:28)). We are made just or righteous through God's grace by the redemption of Jesus (Rm 5:18). It was Paul's wish that the Philippians might be "filled with the fruit of righteousness that comes through Jesus Christ for the glory and praise of God" (Ph 1:11). So we see that in all these Biblical passages, the words, justice and just, have a very comprehensive meaning. They are qualities of the man or woman who obeys the law of God in its entirety, who is morally upright in the sight of God.

On this occasion, however, I wish to speak to you about justice insofar as the just person gives everyone what is rightfully his or hers. We find this meaning in the Bible too. For example, in the Old Testament, a just weight or measure was one that was exact (Dt 25:15); a just judge was one who showed no partiality (Lv 19:15); and justice was the fulfillment of the rights of others (Ex 23:6-8). The prophets condemned those who took bribes, oppressed the innocent (Am 5:11-15), and defrauded the laborer of his wages (Jr 22:13). In all these passages justice means giving everyone what is rightfully his or hers. And it is in this sense that I understand the words, justice and just, here and now.

At the outset, I must make some distinctions. Catholic theologians distinguish two kinds of justice, general and particular.

General justice is that which motivates a citizen to do his or her duty to the *community*. Thus, a citizen practices general justice when he or she obeys the laws of the state, pays taxes, votes, serves in public office, and so on. General justice is also called social justice.

Particular justice is that which motivates a person or community to deal fairly with *individuals.* This again is twofold, distributive and commutative.

Distributive justice motivates civil authorities to spread the burdens and benefits of society among its members in accordance with their needs and capacity to contribute. Accordingly, the rich should pay a greater percentage of their income in taxes than the poor do; only healthy young men should be drafted into the armed forces; the blind and the aged should be given special consideration, and so on. These are examples of distributive justice. The equality involved in distributive justice is said to be geometric or proportional.

On the other hand, *commutative justice* governs the rights and obligations of individuals toward each other. For example, if I pay $5000 for a used automobile worth $5000, then both the dealer and I have acted justly. If, however, I hire a worker for $10 an hour and I pay her only $8 an hour, then I have acted unjustly, and I am bound to make restitution — to give the worker what is coming to her. These are examples of transactions involving commutative justice. The equality involved in commutative justice is said to be arithmetic.

The Catholic teaching about justice has consistently rooted justice in human rights. These, in turn, flow from the dignity of the human person which is rooted in the fact that he or she is made in the image and likeness of God (Gn 1:26-27). The dignity of human beings has been enhanced by the fact that every individual has been redeemed by the death and resurrection of the Son of God.

Catholic teaching has more to say about human rights. *First*, if one has a right, there is a corresponding duty to use one's right properly with respect for the rights of others. For example, if I exercise my right to drive an automobile, I have the corresponding duty to drive safely without endangering the lives of others. *Secondly*, there is a hierarchy of rights; that is to say, some rights are more important than others. For example, a starving person's right to food is far more important than another's right to a luxury item. The more a right is necessary to ensure human dignity, the higher or more important it is. *Third*, a person may have a right in charity, if not in justice. For example, a man in grave need has a right to help from those who can assist him without grave inconvenience, but it is a right in charity only. Sometimes, therefore, charity or love creates a right and obligation where justice does not.

It is evident that we use different criteria to determine what is right and just. For example, most people would agree that the pilot of a commercial aircraft is entitled to greater remuneration than a flight attendant because the pilot has far greater responsibility. In this case we are using the criterion of merit to determine what is right and just. Most people would agree, I think, that blind people should receive special help from society. In this case we are using the criterion of need. Most people would agree that rich and poor are entitled to equal protection under the law. In this case we are appealing to the equality of human beings in the eyes of God to determine what is right and just.

Even with a thorough understanding of the theory of justice and rights, it is often difficult to determine what is just in a particular instance. For example, these questions arise, and it is not always easy to say what is just: To what extent do private clubs have the right to determine qualifications for membership? Is it right for the executives of a company to receive large bonuses while many employees receive only the minimum wage? Should police and fire departments favor minority applicants over other qualified applicants in order to make up for past discrimination? Is it just that the developed nations of the world should consume a disproportionate share of the world's resources? People of good will will answer these questions differently even though they wish to be fair and just. Sometimes one's answer will depend upon the fact that he or she benefits or suffers from the situation. Sometimes civil law will intervene to determine what is fair and just, and in this case the law must be obeyed.

I must note very quickly that animals do not have rights as human beings do. Animals were not created in the image of God; they do not have a spiritual soul and free will or an immortal destiny. They were created expressly for the benefit of human beings (Gn 1:24). Therefore, they may be used as food and as objects of medical experimentation. To cause an animal useless suffering, however, is an abuse of a creature.

There has been, I believe, a growing awareness of what is right and just. There is a greater consciousness of human dignity reflected in the constitutions of many national and international bodies and there have been vigorous efforts to secure the rights of minorities. Still, the pursuit of justice for all is a tough, never-ending task. It will not be won in a day, and it requires more than a halfhearted effort.

QUESTIONS FOR REVIEW

1. What is the meaning of the words, justice and just, in the Bible?
2. What are the different kinds of justice?
3. What is the basis of one's right to justice?
4. How are one's rights qualified?
5. What criteria do we use to determine what is right and just?
6. Why do people of good will disagree about what is just in certain circumstances?
7. Do animals have rights?

CHAPTER 37

Justice (II)
ECONOMIC JUSTICE

On the last occasion I began to speak to you about the teaching of the Catholic Church on justice. A just person, as I am using the term now, gives everyone what is rightfully his or hers. Throughout the course of its long history the Catholic Church has spoken about many issues of justice; but on this occasion I am concerned with modern issues. Let me begin by citing a document written by Pope Leo XIII at the end of the nineteenth century. The document begins with the Latin words, *Rerum Novarum.*

When Leo XIII wrote *Rerum Novarum* in 1891, the industrial revolution was well underway. It had begun in Great Britain in the late eighteenth century and soon spread to other countries including the United States. The worker was simply part of the cost of producing goods, and his rights were largely disregarded. You will recall that Karl Marx, the founder of modern Communism, wrote his famous work, *Das Kapital* (1867), to explain the distress of the working classes at this time. Historically, Marx believed, human labor benefited primarily the nonlaboring classes in the form of capital, while the laborers received little more in wages than their subsistence.

Pope Leo also dealt with the hard lot of the laboring classes. He set down two obligations of employers. The first obligation of the employer is to respect the human dignity of his employees and to promote their welfare, both physical and moral. Pope Leo made the dignity of the human worker the basis of the Church's future social teaching. The second basic obligation of the employer is to pay employees a living wage. A living wage is one that is sufficient to provide the essentials of a decent human life for an average-size family. Moreover, women employees, whether married or single, should receive equal pay for equal work.

Forty years later, in 1931, Pope Pius XI took up anew the teaching of Pope Leo XIII in a document beginning with the Latin words, *Quadragesimo Anno.* In this document, Pope Pius XI emphasized once more the dignity of the worker, the responsibility of the state to promote the well-being of all including workers, the need for cooperation and not confrontation between employers and employees, and the principle of subsidiarity whereby a higher authority such as the government should not intervene in matters which can be handled on a lower level.

In 1961 Pope John XXIII published a document beginning with the Latin words *Mater et Magistra.* In this document Pope John XXIII shifted the focus of Catholic social teaching. He emphasized the global aspect of justice and the interdependence of all human beings and nations. He was particularly concerned with the problems of predominantly agricultural economies, and he invited Catholics to join with non-Catholics in the tremendous task of humanizing modern civilization.

It is interesting to note that a remarkable change has taken place. In some ways the oppressed workers in the United States and Europe, championed by Leo XIII and Pius XI, are now the privileged few in comparison with the other workers of the world. Recent Popes have called the workers of the industrialized world to help those less fortunate than themselves.

Two years after *Mater et Magistra*, in 1963, Pope John XXIII published *Pacem in Terris*. Here he drew up a specific list of human rights based on the fact that men and women are persons. Once again he insisted on the need for collaboration among sovereign states because of their mutual dependence. Social progress, order, security, and peace in any one country are necessarily connected with the same things in all other countries.

In 1965 the Second Vatican Council issued a statement known as *Gaudium et Spes*. The Council reviewed all the changes which have occurred in the modern world. It reaffirmed the dignity of human beings in the midst of all the changes. Human beings are becoming more dependent upon each other because of modern technical advances. As a matter of fact, all men and women constitute one human family and are basically equal. Surely there are important differences among human beings, but excessive economic and social differences among them violate the dignity of the human person. The equal dignity of persons demands a more humane and just condition of life for all.

Two years later in 1967, Pope Paul VI published *Populorum Progressio*. In this document he treated social problems with respect to the rising expectations of men and women everywhere. They "seek to do more, know more, and have more in order to be more." Industrialization, technology, and economic relationships should have one objective — to serve the worker and the global community. The Pope denounced the scandal of glaring inequalities among nations and asserted that the superfluous wealth of rich countries should be placed at the service of poor nations. He concluded by appealing for an effective world authority to promote international collaboration.

Then in *Octogesima Adveniens*, published in 1971, Pope Paul VI recognized a new set of problems confronting the modern world. These problems include urbanization, young people, the role of women, discrimination, the right to emigrate, unemployment, the media, and the environment. The Pope acknowledged, however, that men and women of good will would not always agree about the solution to these problems. In any event, two aspirations continue to motivate human beings — the desire for equality and the desire for freedom.

In the same year of 1971, a representative group of Catholic bishops meeting in Rome issued a statement called *Justice in the World.* The bishops wrote: "Action on behalf of justice and participation in the transformation of the world fully appear to us as a constitutive dimension of the preaching of the gospel, and a part of the Church's mission, which is to redeem and liberate the human race by manifesting and realizing God's plan for it." When we realize that "constitutive" means "essential," this is indeed a strong statement. In other words, one is not faithful to the gospel unless one is involved in the struggle for justice. The bishops went on to say that Catholics need to be drawn away from individualism and wasteful consumption of the earth's resources to a global concern for others, especially the poor and the oppressed.

In 1986 the Catholic bishops of the United States wrote a pastoral letter about the American economy. Among the moral principles which guided them in the composition of their pastoral letter were these: Every economic decision and institution must be judged in the light of whether it protects or undermines the dignity of the human person. All people have a right to participate in the economic life of society. For most people this means that all those who are able and willing to work should be able to find a job. And, finally, all members of society have a special obligation to the poor and vulnerable.

In 1987 Pope John Paul II published *Sollicitudo Rei Socialis*. In this document the Pope spoke of the solidarity of the human race which means in this case "that the good to which we are all called and the happiness to which we all aspire cannot be obtained without an effort and commitment on the part of all." He spoke, too, of sinful social structures which oppress the poor and are the result of an all-consuming desire for profit and the thirst for power on the part of some.

One of the central themes of Catholic social teaching in the documents I have cited is the urgency of economic justice. Both the Church and the world must get on immediately with the task of securing justice for all. Too many men, women, and children do not have what they need to live decent human lives. The relatively prosperous and developed nations of the world have a duty to respond to this need. The underdeveloped nations are like the poor man in the parable of the Good Samaritan. "Who was neighbor to the man who had been despoiled by the robbers?" Jesus asked the lawyer. The answer came, "The one who treated him with compassion." Jesus said to him, "Then go and do the same" (Lk 10:36-37).

The need for economic justice is urgent not only because so many human beings are deprived of the necessities of life, but also because of the danger of war, whose horror and perversity have been greatly magnified by science and technology. One of the main causes of war is the rebellion of people against the injustices they experience. Peace is not the mere absence of war, nor is it a precarious balance of power between enemies. Peace is the work of justice, built up day after day in pursuit of the order intended by God. Pope Paul VI wrote: "We wish to remind all how crucial the present moment is. . . . At stake are the survival of so many innocent children and the access of so many families to conditions fit for human beings. At stake are the peace of the world and the future of civilization. It is time for all peoples to face up to their responsibilities."[1]

1 *Populorum Progressio* no. 80.

QUESTIONS FOR REVIEW

1. What is the basis of Catholic social teaching?
2. How has Catholic teaching about economic justice developed over the years?
3. Why is the establishment of economic justice so urgent?

CHAPTER 38

Justice (III)
ECONOMIC JUSTICE (Cont'd)

The Second Vatican Council spoke of the ever-growing interdependence among all peoples. As a result, the common good of all peoples, that is to say, the fulfillment of their needs, depends upon their cooperation in developing and sharing the goods of this earth. No country ought to go it alone without taking into consideration the needs, aspirations, and welfare of other countries.[1] We see examples of this interdependence on all sides. The amount of interest charged by American banks to Third World countries determines how much of their gross national product goes to service their debts and how much goes to promote internal development. The demand for oil in industrialized countries drives up the price of oil on world markets, so that poor countries must pay more for the oil needed to run their farm machinery and trucks. The development of technology in advanced countries enables less-advanced countries to utilize their resources to a greater degree. Interdependence among nations is a fact, and it creates new rights and duties to ensure the good of all.

Then there is the matter of "social sin." This idea was expressed at the second general conference of Latin American bishops which met at Medellin, Colombia, in 1968. Pope Paul

1 The Church in the Modern World, nos. 25-27.

VI, who was in attendance, warned Christians that they "cannot be associated with systems and structures which cover up and favor grave and oppressive inequalities among the classes and citizens of one and the same country." The concluding statement of the Medellin conference said that "in many instances Latin America finds itself faced with a situation of injustice that can be called institutionalized violence which violates fundamental rights." Injustice of this nature constitutes "a sinful situation."

In his *Sollicitudo Rei Socialis* (1987), Pope John Paul II returned to the same subject. The poor of the southern hemisphere continue to grapple with ever-deeper poverty. They must endure illiteracy, oppression, dependence, inadequate housing, unemployment, and indebtedness. This sorry condition is often the result of sinful structures which are ways of buying, selling, trading, and fostering development that oppress the poor. These sinful structures are rooted in personal sin and linked to the concrete actions of individuals who introduce and maintain these structures. The Pope went on to identify two sinful attitudes that contribute to the creation of sinful structures, namely, the all-consuming desire for profit and the thirst for power. Only by showing a "preference for the poor" can the "first" and "second" world rescue the poor from poverty and save themselves from themselves.

Another problem that involves justice is that of hunger. It is a problem of massive proportions. About half the world's population is undernourished. Many people are actually starving to death — perhaps as many as ten thousand a week. Yet a number of experts claim that our planet can feed at least three times its present population. There is no instant "cure" for world hunger. Emergency food supplies must be delivered as soon as possible to those who are starving. This is a short-term objective. For the long-term, there is the goal of making each country as self-sufficient as possible in producing food. The hope that all may eat depends in large part on cooperation between governments, on scientific breakthroughs, and on skilled management both in the production and distribution of food. As I said, however, the satisfaction of human hunger is a matter of justice. Every human being has a right to a decent life for which sufficient food is essential.

Generally the Church is unable to offer specific solutions to economic problems. For example, the Church cannot teach farmers how to increase the productivity of their land, nor can the Church determine just rates of taxation. However, without specifying details, the Second Vatican Council urged citizens to participate more actively in politics as a means of redressing social injustice. The Popes have called for changes in trade relations and taxation practices, for aid to underdeveloped countries and a fairer price for their raw materials. Surely the reduction of the arms race would enable the great powers to offer more assistance to needy countries. The Church urges individuals to use private property not only for their own benefit, but for the benefit of all. The Church clearly stresses the social nature of property so that the state can regulate the use of private property for the common good. The goods of this earth are meant for all. Economic activity should be concerned with reducing the glaring inequalities between rich and poor. Finally, the Church urges business enterprises to regard human labor as superior to all other elements of economic activity. (When I speak of the Church in this context, I refer, of course, to the Popes and bishops, the official teachers in the Church.)

One of the most important themes in the social teaching of the modern Church is the idea of development. Pope Paul VI spoke of development as the human, civil, and temporal advancement of human beings who are seeking higher levels of culture and prosperity.[2] On one level, development is liberation from disease, exploitation, social inequalities,

2 Message for Mission Sunday, June 5, 1970.

ignorance, oppressive social structures, and lack of culture.[3] On a higher level, development is a search for a new humanism that will embrace the higher values of love and friendship, of prayer and contemplation, which will permit the fullness of authentic development and a transformation from less human conditions to those which are more human.[4] Progress in the methods of production and in the exchange of goods and services has made the economy an apt means for achieving development in this sense.

A new kind of theology has grown out of the struggle to help the poor. It is called liberation theology. People do not always use the term in the same way. Basically, however, liberation theology starts with the suffering of the poor in so many countries of the world. It examines this suffering in the light of the gospel in order to take effective action. Liberation theologians believe they cannot sit on the sidelines; they must get involved in the struggles of the poor. Only by solidarity with the poor and commitment to their cause, they say, can one gain a true insight into the liberating aspects of the gospel.

Finally, I must say a word about socialism, since more than half the world's population lives under some form of socialist government. In general, socialism is a political and economic system in which the government owns the means of production and supervises the distribution of goods. As in the case of English socialism, it is possible for a Christian to be a socialist. However, the Catholic Church has rejected those forms of socialism which affirm that human society was instituted merely for the sake of material well-being. Pope Paul VI explicitly condemned four principles of Marxist ideology, namely atheistic materialism, setting one social class against

2 Message for Mission Sunday, June 5, 1970.
3 *Populorum Progressio*, no. 21.

another, losing sight of the individual in the collective mass, and denying an eternal destiny to human beings.[5]

I should like to conclude my remarks on this occasion with two quotations. The first is taken from Paul's Second Letter to the Corinthians: "You know the gracious act of our Lord Jesus Christ, that for your sake he became poor although he was rich, so that by his poverty you might become rich. . . . Not that others should have relief while you are burdened, but that as a matter of equality your surplus at the present time should supply their needs, so that their surplus may also supply your needs, that there may be equality" (2 Cor 8:9, 13-15). The second quotation is taken from the writings of Pope Paul VI: "Let us build a world where every man, no matter what his race, religion, or nationality, can live a fully human life."[6]

5 *Octogesima Adveniens*, no. 26.
6 *Ibid.*, no. 38.

QUESTIONS FOR REVIEW

1. How are the peoples of this earth interdependent?
2. What is "social sin"?
3. What is the problem of hunger?
4. How is the Church involved in the solution to economic problems?
5. What is to be said about the idea of development?
6. What is liberation theology?
7. How can a Christian be a socialist?

CHAPTER 39

Justice (IV)
JUSTICE FOR MINORITIES

Justice means giving everyone what is rightly his or hers. Everyone has a right to a decent human life. Moreover, great inequalities among individuals, peoples, and nations are an affront to human dignity, for all men and women are basically equal, inasmuch as all have been made in the image and likeness of God. On this occasion I should like to say something about justice for minorities in the United States. I refer particularly to justice for African, Hispanic, and Native Americans. We shall secure justice for these citizens when they achieve basic equality with other Americans.

When I reflect on the situation of black people, Hispanic and Native Americans in the United States, I tend to think of Jesus' story about the Good Samaritan. You will remember that Jews and Samaritans lived side by side in Palestine during the days of Jesus on this earth. For a number of reasons which I shall not mention Jews and Samaritans were enemies. A Jew was in danger when he passed through a Samaritan town. When a Jew wished to insult someone, he called him a Samaritan. It is against this background that we must understand the story of the Good Samaritan.

One day Jesus wished to teach us that anyone in need is our neighbor and that we ought to help him. So he told the story of the Good Samaritan. A Jew, Jesus said, fell into the hands of robbers. They beat him and left him half dead. No one undertook to help him except a merciful Samaritan. Despite the ill feeling between Jews and Samaritans, the Samaritan took care of the injured man. The Samaritan saw a neighbor when he saw someone who needed his help. Our Lord concluded the story of the Samaritan by saying to all of us, "Go and do likewise" (Lk 10:29-37).

There are many people in the United States who have been gravely injured in the course of events. They are seriously in need of help. A disproportionately large number of them are Hispanic, African, and Native Americans. Many of them do not have a decent place in which to live. They live in the poorest sections of our large cities and rural areas. They suffer from a high unemployment rate. There has been a dismaying growth of jobless, skill-less, and nearly hopeless men and women. There has been a disastrous erosion of family life among many of them. Personally, I am not prepared to point the finger of blame at anyone in contemporary America for this sad situation. The causes are too complex, the changes in modern society are too profound for me to say with conviction that the majority or the minority itself is responsible for the plight of so many people.

But the fact remains that certain minorities have been seriously injured in the course of events. By that very fact, according to the parable of the Good Samaritan, they become neighbors who merit our help. By and large, the modern civil rights movement is thoroughly American because it seeks for minorities only the same privileges that so many other Americans enjoy. By and large, the civil rights movement in America is perfectly compatible with Christianity because it seeks to help someone in distress. Obviously, looting and rioting are not legitimate means of furthering the cause of minorities. But legislation, peaceful demonstrations, education, full employment, and equal opportunity are legitimate means of doing so. The Christian and the Catholic will regard the use of any legitimate means to help injured minorities as a concrete application of the parable of the Good Samaritan.

In 1943 the Catholic bishops of the United States issued a statement calling for the extension of full freedom to all citizens within the confines of our beloved country. Specifically, the bishops spoke about the rights of black people. The statement said in part:

"In the providence of God there are among us millions of fellow citizens of the black race. We owe these fellow citizens, who have contributed so largely to the development of our country, and for whose welfare history imposes on us a special obligation of justice, to see that they have in fact the rights which are given them in our Constitution. This means not only political equality, but also fair economic and educational opportunities, a just share in public welfare projects, good housing without exploitation, and a full chance for the social advancement of their race."

After the Second World War considerable progress was made in achieving these goals. African Americans, brought to this country in slavery, continued their quiet but determined march toward the goal of equal rights and equal opportunity. Great and even spectacular advances were made in obtaining voting rights, good education, better-paying jobs, and adequate housing. Through the efforts of men and women of good will, of every race and creed and from all parts of the nation, the barriers of prejudice and discrimination were slowly but inevitably eroded. Unfortunately, however, it appears that in recent years the issues have become confused, and the march toward justice and equality has been slowed if not halted in some areas.

In a second statement published in 1958 the Catholic bishops of the United States said that "the heart of the race question is moral and religious. It concerns the rights of human beings and our attitude toward our fellow human beings."

The bishops went on to say that "no one who bears the name of Christian can deny the universal love of God for all mankind. When Our Lord and Savior Jesus Christ took on the form of man (Ph 2:7) and walked among us, he taught as the first two laws of life the love of God and the love of other human beings. . . . He offered his life in sacrifice for all mankind. His parting mandate to his followers was to 'teach all nations' " (Mt 28:19).

The bishops added: "Our Christian faith is of its very nature universal. It knows not the distinctions of race, color, or nationhood. The missionaries of the Church have spread throughout the world, visiting with equal impartiality nations such as China and India, whose ancient cultures antedate the coming of the Savior, and the primitive tribes of the Americas. The love of Christ and the love of the Christian knows no bounds."

From these solemn truths the American bishops drew certain conclusions:

"First, we must repeat the principle — embodied in our Declaration of Independence — that all men are equal in the sight of God. By equal we mean that they are created by God and redeemed by his divine Son, that they are bound by his law, and that God desires them as his friends in the eternity of heaven. This fact confers on all men and women human dignity and human rights. . . .

"Secondly, we are bound to love our fellow man. The Christian love of which we speak is not a matter of emotional likes or dislikes. It is a firm purpose to do good to all men, to the extent that ability and opportunity permit."[1]

1 Statement of the Bishops of the United States, "Discrimination and the Christian Conscience," 1958.

It seems to me that one key to the advancement of minorities in this country is education. So many immigrants came to this country with little education. They had only the clothes on their backs and they knew little or no English. Yet, many of these immigrants were determined that their children should get a good education, and they encouraged them to work hard in school. The parents realized that a good education develops one's potential. The result has been that the children of these immigrants have prospered economically and risen to the highest offices in the land. Minorities should make every effort to give their children a good education.

A second key to the advancement of minorities in this country is employment. However, African, Hispanic and Native Americans suffer disproportionately from unemployment. Unemployment has a negative impact on human lives and dignity. The unemployed often come to feel that they are worthless and unproductive. Unemployment gives rise to family quarrels, greater consumption of alcohol, child abuse, spouse abuse, and higher rates of infant mortality. Very few people survive long periods of unemployment without some psychological damage. But when people are employed, they support their families and serve others; they become partners with God in developing his creation; they cultivate their personal resources; and they go outside themselves and beyond themselves.

In a pastoral letter called *Economic Justice for All*, written in 1986, the Catholic bishops of the United States said that our great country should commit itself to a policy of full employment. Everyone has a right to a job. The fiscal and monetary policies of the nation should be aimed at this goal. Moreover, job training programs should be expanded, and new jobs should be created. So much needs to be done to upgrade our cities, roads, educational and recreational facilities. Perhaps a reduced work week and the elimination of overtime should be explored.

In any event, until all men and women, including minorities, live in decent circumstances and enjoy a basic equality with other citizens, the cause of justice has not been served.

QUESTIONS FOR REVIEW

1. What is meant by justice for minorities?
2. How does the parable of the Good Samaritan have a bearing upon this matter?
3. Which minorities in the United States lack basic equality with other Americans?
4. What principles should guide us in our treatment of minorities?
5. What are the keys to the advancement of minorities?

CHAPTER 40

Parents And Children (I)
DUTIES OF CHILDREN

Today let's speak about parents and children. This subject is connected with justice because it has to do with the mutual rights and duties of family members. For the moment I am concerned primarily with the duties of children to their parents.

It is beyond dispute that Jesus took seriously his responsibilities as a son. There is the story in the Gospel of Luke that tells how Jesus and Mary and Joseph had traveled from Nazareth, their home, to the city of Jerusalem to visit the temple. The holy city and the temple fascinated Jesus. Somehow Jesus, who was only twelve years old, got separated from his parents. He was lost, but happily his parents finally found him in the temple safe and sound. We are told that Jesus and his parents went back to Nazareth, and there he was obedient to them. Jesus did what any son or daughter ought to do: he did what his parents told him to do (Lk 2:41-51).

On another occasion, Jesus did battle with the Pharisees. One Pharisaic tradition dictated that a person give a fixed share of his produce to God and only then provide for his family. And it could happen that the Pharisee fed God and starved his parents. The Pharisee evaded his responsibility by giving his parents this explanation: "Any support you might have had from me is dedicated to God" (Mt 15:5). But Jesus pointed the Pharisees to the commandment of Moses, "Honor your father and your mother" (Mt 15:4).

Jesus' reverence for his parents is reflected less directly, but perhaps more profoundly in his teachings. He drew images from the family to make his point. For example, he told a parable about a prodigal son. The father gave his son the freedom to venture into a far country and to be on his own. However, the rebellious son had a disastrous experience in that distant land and decided to return home. While he was yet at a distance, his father saw him and had compassion on him. The father ran to his son, embraced him, and kissed him. Jesus likened God to a waiting father, poised to enfold a son who was unworthy of his love (Lk 15:11-24).

And when Jesus taught his disciples to address God in prayer, he said, "When you pray, say: 'Father, hallowed be your name. . . .' " (Lk 11:1-2; cf. Mt 6:9). Out of the relationship to his parents Jesus drew the image of God and the first word to be spoken in prayer.

Nor can we forget the incident recorded in John's Gospel. In the midst of his agony on the cross Jesus was concerned about his widowed mother Mary. So he entrusted his mother to the beloved disciple who took her into his home (Jn 19:25-27).

With the example of our divine Savior in mind, we can specify the obligations of children to their parents. Children owe their parents obedience. God obliges children to obey their parents. That is the fourth of the Ten Commandments. Parents have a right to obedience from their children. Parents fail in their responsibility if they do not expect it or fail to obtain it. Children commit a sin if they fail to obey their parents. Actually, obedience is a liberating experience for a child, for it frees the child from his own inexperience and ignorance.

There is a story from my early youth which illustrates the value of obedience. When I was a boy, my friends and I used to wade in a natural pool of water some distance from my home.

The pool was near a factory, and the water was not too clean. But it was fun to wade in the cool water on a hot summer day and to have the mud on the bottom ooze through your toes. One day my father came to look at the pool and told me not to wade in it because the water was not clean. I was sorry I could no longer wade in the pool because my friends and I had had so much fun. Still, I obeyed. Later, some of my friends got sores on their legs from the dirty water, and they had to go to the doctor for treatment. I saw that my father had been right, and I was glad that I had obeyed him.

Children owe their parents not only obedience, but also respect. Children manifest respect for their parents in a variety of ways: by speaking and acting reverently in their presence, by accepting corrections readily, by seeking the advice of their parents in important matters, and by bearing the faults of their parents with charity.

Children owe their parents love. This love is manifested by helping their parents, by trying to please them, by praying for them, and by sympathizing with them in their sorrows.

Children should obey their parents as long as they remain under the parental roof or until they reach their majority. Of course, the obligation of children to obey supposes that parents do not command what is wrong. Children must obey the laws of God rather than the commands of men, when such commands are contrary to the laws of God. Ordinarily children should consult their parents about the choice of a vocation, but they are not strictly bound to follow their advice. For example, sons and daughters should ask their parents about taking up a certain profession or work, but the son or daughter must make the final decision. So too in the case of marriage. Sons and daughters should seek the advice of their parents in this important matter, but ultimately it is the son or daughter who must decide whether to marry and whom to marry.

The obligation to respect and love one's parents never ceases. Sons and daughters must demonstrate their love for their parents by helping them when they are old. Aged parents need food, shelter, clothing, and care. When they are sick, they need medical attention. If parents are unable to provide these necessities for themselves, then it is the duty of the children to provide them. Moreover, children should see to it that their parents enjoy more benefits than those provided by an old age pension or Social Security.

Even when they have provided all these things, sons and daughters have not met their entire responsibility to aged parents. In addition, they ought to provide a measure of companionship by regular visits. They ought to manifest a spirit of gratitude and appreciation where their parents are concerned. Elderly parents should be kept informed about family affairs. They ought to be reminded that they are remembered in prayer by their children. Occasionally, the hearts of aged parents should be gladdened by a gift.

Another point. Aged parents need the reception of the sacraments. If they are confined to the home or hospital, the parish priest and the hospital chaplain should be informed about them. Thus, one's parents will be able to go to confession, receive Holy Communion and the anointing of the sick. After the death of their parents, grateful children will carry out their last wishes. They will have Masses offered on their behalf, and they will pray for them.

Young people, as you mature, stay close to your parents. Seek their advice and help. They more than anyone else have your interest at heart. And having lived as long as they have, they have learned a thing or two which they can teach you. They can spare you many a hard knock. There is a story about Mark Twain. When he entered his teens, he thought his father knew very little. When Mark Twain entered his twenties, he was amazed how much his father had learned in the intervening years. Young people, stay close to your parents for your own benefit.

I should like to conclude my remarks with these verses from the Book of Sirach, one of the books of the Catholic Bible:

> The LORD sets a father in honor over his children;
> a mother's authority he confirms over her sons.
> He who honors his father atones for sin;
> he stores up riches who reveres his mother.
> He who honors his father is gladdened by children,
> and when he prays he is heard. . . .
> He who fears the LORD honors his father,
> and serves his parents as rulers.
>
> In word and deed honor your father
> that his blessing may come upon you;. . . .
> His father's honor is a man's glory;
> disgrace for her children, a mother's shame.
> My son, take care of your father when he is old;
> grieve him not as long as he lives.
> Even if his mind fail, be considerate with him;
> revile him not in the fullness of your strength.
> For kindness to a father will not be forgotten,
> it will serve as a sin offering — it will take lasting root.
> In time of tribulation it will be recalled to your advantage,
> like warmth upon frost it will melt away your sins.
> A blasphemer is he who despises his father;
> accursed of his Creator, he who angers his mother
> (Si 3:2-16).

QUESTIONS FOR REVIEW

1. What was the attitude of Jesus toward his parents?
2. What are the obligations of children to their parents?
3. Which obligations never cease?
4. What are the obligations of grown children to their parents?

CHAPTER 41

Parents And Children (II)
DUTIES OF PARENTS

Today I wish to speak to you about the obligations of parents to their children.

It is up to husband and wife to determine the number of children they wish to bring into the world. They will make this decision after taking into account their health, financial resources, the difficulty of previous births, and other considerations. Still, not all means of limiting the size of one's family are legitimate. Abortion and artificial contraception are illegitimate means of limiting the size of one's family, but natural family planning methods are legitimate and effective.

Parents must provide for the physical needs of their children. They must safeguard the life of the child before and after birth. They must provide food, clothing, and a home. They should see to it that their children go to school and learn a trade or profession. And parents ought to make a will.

Even more importantly, parents must provide for the spiritual needs of their children. One of these needs is religious instruction. This instruction ought to begin at an early age even before the child goes to school. A young child should be able to make the Sign of the Cross and say the Our Father and the Hail Mary. A preschooler should be acquainted with Jesus and his mother Mary. Chiefly by their own example, parents ought to teach children to pray at bed and meal times, to go to Mass and receive the sacraments, to respect the truth and the name of God. Ideally the religious instruction begun in the home will be continued in a Catholic school where one is available.

I have mentioned the example of parents. It is difficult to exaggerate the influence of parental example. There is no question in my mind that Catholic parents wish to give their children a good example in every respect. But are they conscious of the many ways in which this is possible, that is to say, by using proper language at all times, by unselfishness, by personal prayer, by scrupulous honesty, by moderation in drink, by consideration of others, and so on? If parents live according to a high standard of morality, then generally their children will too. It is said that most children vote for the political party of their parents. Children reflect the attitude of their parents in other important matters too.

Children aren't greatly different from the parents who gave them life, from the teachers who educate them, and from the public figures who provide models for them. If a child lives with criticism, he learns to condemn. If a child lives with hostility, she learns to fight. If, on the other hand, a child lives with tolerance, he learns to be patient. If a child lives with fairness, he learns justice. If a child lives with security, she learns to have faith. As someone has said, "The Christian knows what every psychologist testifies, that we learn to love not by being told to love, but by being loved."

Raising children should be a matter of teamwork on the part of parents. While mothers and fathers have a distinctive contribution to make to family life, only through teamwork can they fulfill their awesome responsibility. Teamwork means that parents provide a united front to their children, so that children are not confused when father and mother disagree. Teamwork means that a father's responsibility is not only to support his family, but also to assume an active role within the family itself. Teamwork means an eagerness on the part of both parents to lighten each other's burdens.

Psychologists say that the presence and availability of fathers are important to their children. The presence of a father fosters the ability of children to relate to male figures. It gives children a better knowledge of social reality, a clearer conception of themselves, and a greater sense of security.

What's a good father to do in these difficult times?

1) Well, for one thing, a good father loves his children and expresses his love. Any expression of love for a child is important, especially cuddling younger ones and hugging older ones. Many teenagers want to know for sure that their parents love them.

2) A good father is present to his children. There is a story about a father who earned a huge salary at an overseas job. His wife and children could not be with him. Finally the man realized that his family needed him more than they needed his salary. One of the most important things a father can give his children is his time.

3) A good father listens. There is a story about a soldier who returned from Vietnam. He had a lot of bad memories. He had lived with death and survived, but no one seemed terribly interested in what he had done. He used to drink until two or three o'clock in the morning. When he came home, his dad would have a pot of coffee going. They would sit in the dark and talk. Eventually the bitterness left the soldier, and he became a policeman in Los Angeles. A father is one who listens.

4) Finally, a good father sets rules — rules for dating, television, companions, homework, and the like. Children perceive such discipline coupled with the presence of the father as one more expression of caring.

It is especially important for youngsters to know that they are loved. If they don't feel loved at home, they could grow up believing there is no love to be found anywhere. One way to help children feel loved and secure is by providing structure and discipline in their lives. While parents should be flexible, they should also set limits. Of course, there's more to discipline than saying No. The only real discipline comes from love, not fear.

Parents have to remember that children are people too. Children want someone to care for them. They want to be themselves, to be active instead of passive, to give something to the world around them. Like other people, children are going to make mistakes. Too much insistence upon perfection can give children a fear of making mistakes. A child is going to drop a plate. Help him pick it up. Helping youngsters learn how to handle mistakes can teach them self-confidence. In the process parents may also learn to relax and stop demanding an impossible level of perfection from themselves. Parents are people too.

Surely parents are bound to correct their children. Often this duty is a painful one, but it may not be neglected. Children ought to be told plainly what is right and wrong; they ought to be advised how to conduct themselves in a similar situation in the future; then, if necessary, they ought to be punished, but without a display of temper, passion, or cursing, and, of course, without cruelty. Moreover, parents should bear in mind that the correction of teenagers has to be carried out differently than that of younger children.

So many other things parents must do for their children: open the hearts of their children to all men and women despite their race, color, or creed; give older children an opportunity to be heard; give them a zest for learning; teach them a sensible attitude toward money; treat all children with equal affection; answer their questions; don't blame or punish a child in the presence of the children next door; and concentrate on a child's good points, not his failings.

Parents must love their children as a sacred charge entrusted to them by Almighty God. In a sense the immortal souls of children are in the hands of their parents. Sometimes, however, despite the best efforts of parents, a child will go astray. Children retain their free will, and they are subject to influences over which parents have no control. Parents must not blame themselves in this situation. Let them continue to pray for their children, for "the fervent prayer of a righteous person is very powerful" (Jm 5:16).

Finally, parents should not overlook the need of perseverance. I am reminded of the story of Fritz Kreisler, the renowned violinist of another day. On one occasion he was approached by an enthusiastic admirer who said, "Mr. Kreisler, I would give my life to play the violin as you do." Quietly he replied, "Madame, I have done just that." Raising a family requires sacrifice and perseverance. The devoted artist, the struggling writer, the dedicated public servant, all pay a price for whatever they accomplish. Long hours, loneliness, frustration are part of raising a family, but it's worth it.[1]

1 I am indebted to the "Christopher News Notes" for most of the thoughts in this chapter.

QUESTIONS FOR REVIEW

1. How should parents determine the number of children in their family?
2. What should parents do for their children?
3. How should parents act as a team?
4. What can a father in particular do for his children?
5. How should parents correct their children?
6. Why is perseverance needed to raise a family?

CHAPTER 42

HUMAN LIFE (I)

Today I wish to speak to you about human life, a subject having to do with the fifth commandment which obliges us to respect human life and forbids murder. My remarks will have a bearing upon what I say later about warfare, capital punishment, abortion, and euthanasia.

We all know how human beings value their own lives. When life is threatened, they fight tooth and nail, as it were, to preserve it. We all have a deep fear and dread of extinction which produces a spontaneous sense of outrage when human life is wantonly destroyed or manipulated. On the other hand, history records the strenuous efforts of human beings to preserve and strengthen life through public policy, scientific research, and charitable endeavors. In this way, we express our conviction about the value of human life even before we take into account the teaching of religion which emphasizes the sacredness of human life.

Important secular documents recognize the value and dignity of human life. The words of the American Declaration of Independence are well-known: "We hold these truths to be self-evident, that all men are created equal, that they are endowed by their Creator with certain unalienable rights, that among these are life, liberty, and the pursuit of happiness." The preamble of the United Nations Declaration of Human Rights contains these words: "Recognition of the inherent dignity and equal and inalienable rights of all members of the human family is the foundation of freedom, justice, and peace in the world."

Historically, all the great religions of the world have proclaimed the dignity of the human person and human life. The Judeo-Christian tradition has been particularly explicit. In the Book of Genesis we read:

> "God created man in his image;
> in the divine image he created him;
> male and female he created them" (Gn 1:27).

In the preceding verse of the same chapter we are told that man is the image of God in the sense that he has received from God the power to rule over other creatures (Gn 1:26). Human beings are uniquely God's image. And that image resides chiefly in the soul, the spiritual principle of life. Thus, we read in the Book of Wisdom:

> "God formed man to be imperishable;
> the image of his own nature he made him" (Ws 2:23).

Psalm 8 extols the dignity of man:

> "What is man that you should be mindful of him,
> or the son of man that you should care for him?
> You have made him little less than the angels,
> and crowned him with glory and honor.
> You have given him rule over the works of your hands,
> putting all things under his feet" (Ps 8:5-7).

Psalm 139 expresses the wonder of human conception:

> "Truly you have formed my inmost being;
> you knit me in my mother's womb.

> I give you thanks that I am fearfully, wonderfully
> made;
> wonderful are your works.
> My soul also you knew full well;
> nor was my frame unknown to you
> When I was made in secret,
> when I was fashioned in the depths of the earth"
> (Ps 139: 13-15).

The phrase, "depths of the earth," is figurative language for the womb. The psalmist is describing the conception of a human being in the womb of his mother, stressing the hidden, mysterious nature of what goes on there. Isaiah (49:1), Jeremiah (1:15), and Paul (Gal 1:15) all testify that God knew them already in their mothers' womb. There God established with them that personal relationship which all human beings have with their Creator.

In the New Testament Jesus spoke of God's providential care for each one of us: "Are not two sparrows sold for a small coin? Yet not one of them falls to the ground without your Father's knowledge. Even all the hairs of your head are counted. So do not be afraid; you are worth more than many sparrows" (Mt 10:29-30). Each human being is the object of God's concern.

At the Last Supper Jesus made it clear that he was going to shed his blood for all men and women (Mt 26:28; Mk 14:24). At the end of his ministry on this earth, Jesus sent his representatives into the whole world to make disciples of all nations (Mt 28:19). Paul affirmed that all human beings have been redeemed by Christ and called to union with him: "[With the Jews] the Gentiles are coheirs, members of the same body, and copartners in the promise in Christ Jesus through the gospel" (Ep 3:6). The Book of Revelation tells of the ultimate triumph of God's elect. They are "a great multitude, which no one could count, from every nation, race, people, and tongue" (Rv 7:9).

Reviewing these passages, we begin to appreciate the Biblical teaching about the personal dignity of human beings. Men and women are made in the image and likeness of God. They have dominion over other creatures, and they are crowned with glory and honor. God has established a personal relationship with them, and they are the objects of his providential concern. Jesus shed his blood for the redemption of all men and women, and he sent his representatives to preach the gospel to all. All are called to fellowship with God in the eternal kingdom of heaven. Human life is a gift of God of which men and women are the stewards and for which they are responsible to him.

The Biblical teaching about the dignity of the human person and the value of human life was repeated by the Second Vatican Council. According to the Council, all things on earth should be related to men and women as their center and crown. Men and women were created in the image of God, they are capable of knowing and loving their Creator, and they are the masters of all earthly creatures.

The Council went on to say that man is one even though he is made of body and soul. The bodies of men and women are good and honorable since they were created by God, and he will raise them up on the last day. However, men and women have spiritual and immortal souls by which they surpass the material universe and enter into communion with God. Men and women have an eternal destiny.

Further, the Second Vatican Council spoke of the voice of conscience which summons men and women to love good and avoid evil. Conscience is the most secret core and sanctuary of a person. There he or she is alone with God. Men and women enjoy freedom which is an exceptional sign of the divine image within them. Because they are free, human beings are able to seek their Creator spontaneously, and one day they will have to render an account of their actions before the judgment seat of God.

Finally, the bishops of the Council taught that Jesus who is "the image of the invisible God" (Col 1:15), is also the perfect man. By his incarnation the Son of God united himself in some fashion with every man and woman. The assumption of human nature by the Son of God raised that nature to a divine dignity in our respect too. In virtue of his death on the cross, Jesus delivered each one of us from sin, so that we can say with Paul: the Son of God "loved me and gave himself up for me" (Gal 2:20). All this holds true not only for Christians, but for all men and women of good will in whose hearts grace works in an unseen way.[1]

From all this we should understand more clearly, I think, the dignity of the human person, who stands above all things and whose rights and duties are inviolable.[2] Indeed, the dignity and value of a human person precedes and overshadows whatever an individual may accomplish. Too often we attribute value to human life only in terms of what one makes, does, accomplishes, or possesses. No, living human beings are gifted in their very being, prior to what they succeed in doing or producing. Human persons possess an equal and inherent value not from what they do, but from who they are — children of God, made in his image and likeness and redeemed by his divine Son.

Have you ever seen the picture of a little boy in ragged clothes? He is standing in front of a ramshackle house in a rural setting. At the bottom of the picture is the caption: "God made me, and God don't make junk." That's my point exactly.

1 Constitution on the Church in the Modern World, pt. 1, ch. 1.
2 *Ibid.*, no. 25.

QUESTIONS FOR REVIEW

1. How do individuals testify to the value of human life?
2. What do some important secular documents say about the value of human life?
3. What does the Bible say about this matter?
4. What did the Second Vatican Council teach about the dignity of the human person?
5. How does the dignity of human beings precede what they accomplish?

CHAPTER 43

Human Life (II)
WARFARE AND CAPITAL PUNISHMENT

On this occasion I wish to continue my discussion of the value of human life by speaking about the destruction of human life in war and by capital punishment.

Can we reconcile the wholesome killing of human beings in warfare with respect for human life? The answer of the Church is a guarded Yes. A nation is permitted to defend itself against unjust aggression. We are not obliged to accept every injustice, every injury which others would inflict on us. In other words there is such a thing as a just war waged in defense of one's legitimate rights. The bishops of the Second Vatican Council taught: "As long as the danger of war persists and there is no international authority with the necessary competence and power, governments cannot be denied the right of lawful self-defense, once all peace efforts have failed."[1]

Having admitted the possibility of a just war in defense of one's rights, we must note at once the conditions for a just war. 1) A just war is undertaken as a last resort to correct or resist a very serious injustice. 2) A just war is authorized by the government of a nation which is responsible for the

1 Constitution on the Church in the Modern World, no. 79.

common good; it cannot be authorized by individuals. 3) A just war is fought with hope of success, that is to say, with hope of rectifying the injustice. If there is no hope of success, then a war is unjustified. 4) A just war achieves some good which outweighs the killing and destruction.

Further, 5) a just war is not waged against civilians. "Every act of war directed at the indiscriminate destruction of whole cities or vast areas with their inhabitants is a crime against God and man, which merits firm and unequivocal condemnation."[2] By this declaration the bishops of the Second Vatican Council seem to rule out the use of high megaton bombs in densely populated areas, since such bombs would kill millions of innocent civilians. This outright rejection of indiscriminate and total warfare on civilian populations does not of itself rule out all use of nuclear weapons. Still, any use of nuclear weapons, even on a limited scale, runs the risk of total warfare and the danger of a world holocaust. Probably it is more difficult to justify warfare in the nuclear age than ever before.

Because a nation has a right to self-defense, those who serve in the armed forces deserve our gratitude and appreciation. They are defenders of freedom and security. Indeed, they make war less likely because the capacity to defend oneself discourages attacks by others. In this way men and women of the military make a genuine contribution to peace.

What about those who refuse to serve in the armed forces of their country? They may refuse to do so because they object to warfare as such or to the legitimacy of a particular war. Granted the complexity of moral judgments about modern warfare, one can understand how some persons, called conscientious objectors, could take such a stance. The bishops of the Second Vatican Council said this: "It seems that just laws should make humane provision for the case of conscientious

2 *Ibid.*, no. 80.

objectors who refuse to carry arms, provided they accept some other form of community service."[3]

The bishops of the Second Vatican Council firmly condemned the arms race, that is to say, the efforts of countries large and small to increase their stockpile of nuclear and conventional weapons. The bishops said somewhat gloomily: "There is every reason to fear that if the arms race continues, it will bring forth those lethal disasters which are in preparation." Furthermore, the bishops saw the arms race as actually creating the unjust conditions which precipitate wars: "As long as extravagant sums of money are poured into the development of new weapons, it is impossible to deal adequately with the misery that prevails in the world at the present time."[4] The Second Vatican Council did not call for unilateral disarmament, but it clearly insisted on the obligation to expend every effort to achieve bilateral disarmament.

Besides disarmament, another means of reducing the danger of war is to struggle for justice. One of the main causes of war is the rebellion of people against the injustices they experience. Peace is not the mere absence of war nor a precarious balance of power between enemies. Peace is the work of justice, built up day after day in pursuit of the order intended by God. True peace will be achieved when men and women have enough to eat and are able to chart their own destiny free from outside domination and exploitation.

Then there is the destruction of human life by capital punishment. Capital punishment may be defined as the imposition of the death penalty by the state. It was widely used in ancient times. It is found in the Code of Hammurabi (c. 1750 B.C.), a king of Babylon. Methods of capital punishment included beheading, stoning, impaling, drowning, and burning. From the fall of Rome to the beginning of the modern era,

3 *Ibid.*, no. 79.
4 *Ibid.*, no. 81.

capital punishment was practiced throughout Western Europe. The modern movement for the abolition of the death penalty began in the 18th century with the writings of Montesquieu and Voltaire. Since then the movement has continued to gain strength worldwide. In 1972 the Supreme Court struck down the arbitrary and inconsistent imposition of the death penalty in the United States, but it left the way open for Congress and state legislatures to enact new capital punishment laws in the future.

The Old Testament clearly authorized capital punishment for such crimes as blasphemy, false worship, kidnapping, striking or cursing parents, adultery, incest, homosexual actions, and bestiality (Ex 21:12-17; 22:19; Lv 20:9-16). Paul acknowledged the right of the state to carry the sword, that is to say, to punish criminals, but he did not speak explicitly of the death penalty (Rm 13:4). From the beginning, the Catholic Church has recognized the right of the state to execute criminals. St. Thomas Aquinas (1225-1274) formulated the traditional teaching when he wrote: "If a person is dangerous and destructive to the community on account of some sin, it is praiseworthy and healthy that he be killed in order that the common good be preserved."[5] In other words, just as the state has the right to protect its citizens against an external enemy by going to war, so the state has the right to protect its citizens against an internal enemy by capital punishment. In the latter case, capital punishment may be compared to the amputation of a diseased limb to save the whole body.

Granted, then, the right of society to take the life of a criminal, we must ask: Should it do so? The Church as a whole has been slow to answer this question. However, those who favor the abolition of capital punishment advance several arguments in support of their position:

1) Society, they say, no longer needs to take the life of a

5 *Summa Theologiae* 2a2ae.64.2.

criminal to protect itself. We have other ways of protecting ourselves. Because we do not have to take life, we should not.

2) Punishment should be medicinal and rehabilitative. The punishment of a criminal should aim at the reeducation and reintegration of the guilty person into society in accordance with his human dignity. Capital punishment excludes such an effort.

3) Those who favor capital punishment believe it deters criminals; yet there is no convincing evidence that it does. Surely capital punishment does not deter those who commit crimes of passion, nor those criminals who hope to escape detection and conviction.

4) Statistics show that the death penalty is inflicted disproportionately on poor people and minorities who do not have the legal resources available to the affluent. If the method of inflicting the death penalty is unfair to particular groups, then it does not safeguard the common good and public justice.

5) Sometimes innocent persons are put to death. In this case the injustice cannot be rectified.

6) The Lord enjoined upon Christians the duty to love one's enemies (Mt 5:43-44).

A position paper prepared by the Pontifical Commission for Justice and Peace linked the Catholic Church's traditional opposition to abortion and euthanasia to the issue of capital punishment. This paper suggested that Catholics show respect for life in every situation whether it be the life of the unborn or the life of the elderly or the life of the criminal. Surely there is a radical difference between the unborn and aged on the one hand and the criminal on the other. It is the difference between innocence and guilt. Still, respect for life in all its forms creates an atmosphere in which innocent life, however helpless it may be, can flourish.[6]

6 *Origins*, Dec. 9, 1976, 6, 392.

QUESTIONS FOR REVIEW

1. How can killing in war be justified?
2. What are the conditions for a just war?
3. May a nation use nuclear weapons to defend itself?
4. How should we regard those who serve in the armed forces?
5. Do conscientious objectors to warfare do justice to their country?
6. What are the moral objections to the arms race?
7. Why does the state have the right to take the life of a criminal?
8. What are the arguments for the abolition of the death penalty?

CHAPTER 44

Human Life (III)
ABORTION AND EUTHANASIA

I have already spoken about taking human life in war and by capital punishment. Now I wish to say something about taking human life by abortion and euthanasia.

Induced abortion may be defined as the deliberate destruction of the fetus before it is viable. In contrast to capital punishment, the victim of abortion is completely innocent. Christian tradition has often compared abortion and infanticide.

The twentieth century has generally seen the relaxation of restrictions against abortion. In 1973, the United States Supreme Court ruled that a state may not prevent a woman from having an abortion during the first six months of pregnancy. Thus the Supreme Court invalidated abortion laws in some states and overturned restrictive abortion laws in many other states. As one supporter of the Court's decision put it, the Court declared that "a woman has a constitutional right to a dead fetus." Abortion was legalized in England in 1967 and is also permitted in the Soviet Union, Japan, China, Scandinavia, and elsewhere. Abortion procedures include vacuum suction, dilation, and scraping as well as saline injection and hysterotomy.

As far as I know, the Old Testament does not explicitly treat of abortion. However, the Biblical reverence for life, for children, and for God's mysterious role in procreation, could never tolerate abortion in a permissive way. It was something totally alien to the Jewish mind. Nor does the New Testament explicitly treat of abortion. However, the love of Christ for little children (Lk 18:15-17) and his personal identification with the least of his brethren (Mt 25:40, 45) seem incompatible with either infanticide or abortion. Furthermore, the New Testament presents Jesus as truly human from the moment of his conception, for Elizabeth proclaimed the presence of the Lord in Mary's womb immediately after the annunciation (Lk 1:43).

In Christian tradition the condemnation of abortion has been explicit from the very first century. For example, the *Didache* or *The Teaching of the Twelve Apostles*, a work emanating from a Christian community in Syria, lays down this precept: "You shall not murder a child by abortion nor kill that which is begotten."[1] Subsequently, the Fathers and councils of the Church condemned the practice with one voice. The Second Vatican Council in the 1960's declared concisely and firmly: "Life must be protected with the utmost care from the moment of conception: abortion and infanticide are abominable crimes."[2] The law of the Catholic Church applies an automatic excommunication to those who procure an abortion.[3] The purpose of such a severe penalty is to reinforce the Church's teaching about respect for the lives of tiny and helpless human beings.

Modern science confirms the distinct humanity of the child in the womb. It teaches that a totally new living being begins with the fertilization of the egg by the sperm. The egg has only half the number of genes and chromosomes as the normal cell. The full complement is achieved on fertilization by the sperm which also has only half the normal number of

1 *Didache*, 2, 25.
2 Constitution on the Church in the Modern World, no. 51.
3 *Code of Canon Law*, c. 1398.

genes and chromosomes. The union of sperm and egg produces a totally new being distinct from the mother. Thereafter the fertilized egg or zygote directs its own development from within just like any human being. The zygote undergoes cell division, resulting in the formation of tissues and organs. The life process, which began at fertilization, is continuous through implantation, quickening, viability, and beyond, until death. Destruction of life in the womb is destruction of a distinct human life.

Catholic theologians distinguish between direct and indirect abortion. Direct abortion, such as craniotomy or embryotomy, is a straightforward attack on innocent human life and always forbidden. Indirect abortion is the death of a fetus as the side effect of an operation aimed directly at curing a pathological condition in the mother. Let us say, for example, that the life of an expectant mother is threatened by a cancerous uterus or a fallopian tube about to rupture. In this case, it is permissible to employ a medical procedure aimed at curing the pathological condition even if it results in the death of the fetus. In saying this, I am employing what is known as the principle of double effect which is widely recognized in the Catholic Church. The direct effect of the operation is to save the mother's life which compensates for the indirect effect of killing the fetus.

Suppose there's a likelihood that a child will be born deformed or retarded. Even in this case the child in the womb may not be killed. A deformed or retarded child retains its human dignity, and its life can be meaningful to others. Many people assume that no family in its right mind would adopt a retarded child. That's just not true. There are families with a Christian or humanistic motivation who want to adopt a child not because of anything the child might do for them, but just because the child needs help.

Then there is the matter of euthanasia, which is the act or practice of killing individuals who are hopelessly sick or injured for reason of mercy. Euthanasia is voluntary when a suffering person permits or even demands the termination of his or her life. Euthanasia is involuntary when others decide to end the life of a suffering person.

The Judeo-Christian tradition has never accepted voluntary or involuntary euthanasia. The Old Testament stressed the inviolability of the innocent, for we read in the Book of Exodus: "The innocent and the just you shall not put to death" (Ex 23:7). The New Testament mandates Christians to love others as themselves (Lk 10:27) and to treat the least of Christ's brothers and sisters as Christ himself (Mt 25:40). Surely such a mandate requires unselfish care of suffering and helpless individuals.

The bishops of the Second Vatican Council reaffirmed the Church's opposition to euthanasia. They rejected whatever is opposed to life itself, and they mentioned such crimes as murder, genocide, abortion, euthanasia, and suicide. The bishops concluded their statement by saying: "All these things and the like are criminal: they poison human society, but they do more harm to those who practice them than to those who suffer from the injury. Moreover these things are a supreme dishonor to the Creator."[4]

Often euthanasia is seen as the only alternative to severe and unrelieved suffering in a patient who is terminally ill. However, contemporary medicine, especially as it is practiced in the hospice programs for the terminally ill, can relieve severe suffering for almost all patients. Proper pain medication and attention to the psychological effects of terminal illness can ease the burden of suffering considerably without shortening life.

While we may do nothing to hasten death, we are not obliged to use every conceivable means to forestall death.

4 Constitution on the Church in the Modern World, no. 27.

Since the seventeenth century at least, Catholic theologians have made a distinction between the ordinary and extraordinary means of prolonging life. This distinction is based on common sense and the Biblical notion of responsible stewardship of human life. We are bound to use the ordinary means of preserving life, but we are not bound to use the extraordinary means of preserving life. What is the meaning of this distinction?

We are bound to use the ordinary means of preserving life. The ordinary means are those which lie at hand and are in common use among doctors and surgeons, and consist of those medicines, treatments, and operations which offer a reasonable hope of benefit and do not involve excessive pain, expense, or hardship. In the average community today ordinary means would include intravenous feeding, blood transfusions, the use of oxygen, and routine operations and amputations, even major ones.

However, we are not bound to use the extraordinary means of preserving human life. Extraordinary means are those which entail great hardship, suffering, or expense, or those which offer little hope of success — for example, drastic operations on the brain and the implantation of a human heart. The use of extraordinary means is not mandatory, but optional.

It will always be true that in matters of genuine doubt one should consider a procedure ordinary and obligatory, rather than the contrary. Fortunately, when life is at stake, the human instinct is to seek help over and above the hazy minimum that morality rigorously demands.

QUESTIONS FOR REVIEW

1. What does the Bible say about abortion?
2. What does modern science say about the beginning of human life?

3. What is the difference between direct and indirect abor tion? When is the latter permitted?
4. What is euthanasia? Why is it wrong?
5. What is the difference between ordinary and extraordinary means of preserving life?
6. How far must we go to preserve human life?

CHAPTER 45

HUMAN HEALTH

I have just concluded my series of talks about the dignity and sanctity of human life. Now I wish to take up a related subject dealing with human health. What is our responsibility for our own health and the health of others? If the fifth of the Ten Commandments obliges us to care for our own life and the life of others, surely it obliges us to care for the gift of health so that life may continue and be enhanced.

What is health? Health means soundness in body, mind, or spirit. Health includes freedom from disease and pain. We speak of a healthy baby, a healthy child, a healthy adult. A person with cancer is sick, not healthy. Health is also a mental state. A person in an insane asylum is not a healthy person. Health is a desirable condition of the whole person.

If health is a condition of the whole person, then the attempt to preserve health and to regain it when it has been lost should include moral and spiritual care as well as physical and psychological care. The reasonable pursuit of health and healing involves personal efforts and professional help.

"This includes personal responsibility to seek a balanced and nutritious diet, to take adequate exercise, to achieve a proper blend of work and play, and to overcome anxieties and tensions which undermine health. It also includes the seeking of competent medical, psychological, moral, and spiritual help to maintain health. It involves a personal responsibility to use reliable medications and medical procedures which were discussed on another occasion as the ordinary means of prolonging life."[1]

We Americans tend to be apathetic and unmotivated regarding our own health. Quite commonly we believe that illness is a matter of random chance or fate. In fact, personal lifestyles are greatly responsible for unnecessary disease and disability. Some years ago the Surgeon General of the United States recommended certain simple steps that we can all take to preserve health and reduce the chance of accident: 1) stop smoking cigarettes, 2) cut down the use of alcohol, 3) reduce the intake of fats, salt, and sugar in the diet, 4) get regular exercise, 5) have periodic health check-ups, and 6) observe speed laws and wear seat belts when driving.

Surely the abuse of tobacco, alcohol, and drugs is inconsistent with the obligation to care for one's health. The dangers of heavy and prolonged smoking to one's health are generally recognized. The heavy use of alcohol and other drugs can seriously impair one's health. The sad thing is that so many young people in our society abuse tobacco and drugs. I would encourage them to stop using them completely. Society needs the full measure of their health, idealism, and consciousness to deal with its problems. The preservation of health requires some planning, sacrifice, and self-discipline on our part. Good health may often be not so much the result of luck or fate or an unmerited gift of God, but the natural reward of virtue.

In connection with the need to care for one's health, I should like to say a word about five different matters, namely, surgery, organ transplants, the determination of death, mental health, and medical experimentation.

First, a word about surgery. In many cases surgery has become a routine and safe procedure for safeguarding human

1 D. McCarthy in E. Gratsch (ed.), *Principle of Catholic Theology* (Staten Island: Alba House, 1981), 350-351.

health. The removal of diseased organs and malignant tumors is quite legitimate since we are allowed to sacrifice one part of the body for the good of the whole. The principle involved here is known as the principle of totality according to which the good of the part is subordinated to the good of the whole.

What is to be said about the transplant of organs from one human body to another? The giving of organs (such as a kidney) or non-functional tissue (like the cornea of a blind eye) from one person to another is justified on the grounds that it is an act of love. As a general principle, however, the benefit to the recipient should be proportionate to the harm done to the donor. Moreover, the gift of an organ should not deprive the donor of life nor of the functional integrity of his body. Organs may be transplanted from an animal to a human body if they are compatible. One may also donate his or her body after death for transplant use.

What is to be said about the determination of death? When is a person truly dead? So that they can obtain organs such as kidneys and hearts as "fresh" as possible for transplantation, physicians and surgeons are concerned about the determination of death. The verification of death does not fall within the competence of the Church. We may say, however, that "if the signs of life like breathing and blood circulation are being maintained without the unifying internal function of the patient's central nervous system, they are not true signs of human life and the patient is really dead. . . . On the other hand, if the life support system is truly supporting the internal life process and the central nervous system continues to function, the patient should not be declared dead."[2]

Needless to say, we must cultivate the health of both mind and body. Mental illness, like physical illness, is an obstacle to health. Mental illness is more complex to treat. In dealing with mental illness we must recognize the role of human

2 *Ibid.*, 352.

freedom and moral weakness. Today chemical and behavioral treatments are more common than surgical operations to cure mental illness. In all such cases, the patient must consent freely and in an informed manner to the prescribed treatment, and the benefit to the sick person must be proportionate to the risk entailed.

The greatest single form of mental illness today is addiction to tobacco and drugs, especially alcohol. I think it is accurate to say that one who is addicted to a drug suffers from a loss of freedom. The addict may experience an attraction for a drug that is well-nigh irresistible when he is left to himself. The addict becomes less and less capable of perceiving alternatives to his addiction; hence, he cannot help acting as he does. Often he will be excused from grave moral fault. The real moral responsibility of the addict is to seek help from others. Therapy for addiction can be highly successful, but in many cases control is assured only through complete abstinence.

Finally, there is another matter about which I should like to say a word: medical experimentation on human beings for the purpose of improving health. Some experimentation can be carried out usefully on animals, but there must be experimentation on human beings too if progress is to be made. In all cases, the patient must consent to the experimentation, since the doctor has only that authority over the patient which the latter gives him. Moreover, the patient is not the absolute master of his or her body. He or she may not, therefore, dispose of themselves entirely as they see fit.

There are two kinds of experimentation on patients. One kind of experimentation is undertaken for the benefit of the patient under treatment. If a sure remedy is available, it should ordinarily be employed. Where, however, no sure remedy is available, the patient may take a risk in proportion to the gravity of the illness. A person dying of cancer might well consent to an experimental treatment that involves a high risk.

The other kind of experimentation on patients is undertaken for the benefit of others. The duty of loving other human beings permits a limited degree of risk to life or bodily integrity for the sake of others. How far then may one go? In 1954, Pope Pius XII said that a person "has no right to permit scientific or practical experiments which entail *serious injury* or threaten to *impair his or her health.*"[3] In the same context he ruled out experiments which could conceivably result in mutilation or death.

May an authorized person give proxy consent for medical experimentation upon children or the comatose or the unborn? Some say Yes, and some say No. Those who say Yes argue that even incompetent persons can be expected to make a contribution to the good of the human race, provided only a minimal risk is involved. Those who say No argue that incompetent persons must be treated as persons and not as animals. Moreover, they cite the danger of interpreting minimal risk to incompetent persons ever more widely.

We all know what progress modern medicine is making. New procedures and new medical possibilities will raise new questions. Surely the principles and values about which I have been speaking will have new applications in the future. Meanwhile, it seems to me that the major concern for most of us in this area should be the preservation of our own health and the prevention of disease. For many of us this will mean a considerable change in our lifestyles. We are often the victims of our own careless habits. Greater attention to our health, while we still enjoy it, will result in happier and more productive lives in the long run. The duty to preserve human health is closely bound up with the insistence of God's fifth commandment that we preserve human life.

3 Cf. *The Human Body* (Boston: Daughters of St. Paul, 1960). Italics added.

QUESTIONS FOR REVIEW

1. What is health?
2. How can we preserve our health?
3. Why may a surgeon remove a diseased organ or limb?
4. How can the transplantation of bodily organs be justified?
5. When is a person truly dead?
6. How is mental illness treated?
7. What is the responsibility of those addicted to drugs or alcohol?
8. When is medical experimentation on human beings justified?

CHAPTER 46

Human Sexuality (I)
BIBLICAL TEACHING

Today I wish to take up the sixth and ninth of God's Ten Commandments: "Thou shalt not commit adultery" and "Thou shalt not covet thy neighbor's wife." These commandments have to do with human sexuality. In these remaining talks I am concerned with human sexuality, a very broad subject indeed. On this occasion I should like to answer just one question: What does the Bible teach about human sexuality?

The Biblical teaching about human sexuality begins with the two stories of creation in the Book of Genesis. In the first story, the author tells us that God created man and woman in his own image, giving them dominion over the rest of creation. And he gave them this command: "Be fertile and multiply; fill the earth and subdue it" (Gn 1:27-28). In the second story, the author tells us that God wished to find a suitable partner for man among all the creatures that God had created. So God formed a woman that the man might not be alone. The author goes on to say, "That is why a man leaves his father and mother and clings to his wife, and the two of them become one body" (Gn 2:24). The sacred writer stresses the fact that the conjugal union is willed by God. These stories express the two important purposes of marriage and sexual activity: they unite husband

and wife for their mutual assistance and enable them to multiply and fill the earth.

The goodness and value of the sexual relationship in marriage were never in doubt as far as the Israelites were concerned. Children were the greatest blessing God could bestow on a marriage. Children prevented one's name from being "blotted out from Israel" (Dt 25:6). The lack of children was a cause for sorrow (1 S 1:1-20). The psalmist congratulated the just man to whom the Lord had given a fruitful wife and sturdy children (Ps 128:1-4).

What is more, the Israelites were quite aware of the other blessings of the marital union, namely, companionship and mutual assistance. There is the story of Elkanah and his wife Hannah. Before the birth of their son Samuel, Hannah complained to her husband that she had no children from him, but he replied to her: "Am I not more to you than ten sons?" (1 S 1:5-8). The Book of Proverbs advises the married man:

> "Have joy of the wife of your youth,
> Your lovely hind, your graceful doe.
> Her love will invigorate you always,
> Through her love you will flourish continually,
> When you lie down she will watch over you,
> And when you wake, she will share your concerns;
> Wherever you turn, she will guide you" (Pr 5:18-20).

The law of Israel exempted a newly married man from military service for one year, so that he might "bring joy to the wife he has married" (Dt 24:5).

It was the prophet Hosea in the eighth century B.C. who was the first to describe the relation between Yahweh and Israel in terms of a marriage. According to this image, Israel's worship of false gods was characterized as adultery.

It is true that polygamy, which was the practice of having several wives at one time, did exist among the chosen people, especially among the kings and nobles. David, for example, had a number of wives (2 S 3:2-5). Solomon had hundreds of wives and concubines (1 K 11:3). The desire for progeny was largely responsible for the practice. However, as we have seen, the creation stories in the Book of Genesis and the Wisdom literature of the Bible propose monogamy as the ideal state; and after the exile (587-537 B.C.) polygamy practically disappeared.

Divorce was taken for granted in the Old Testament, and the Book of Deuteronomy tried to mitigate its evil effects (Dt 24:1). Apparently only the husband had the right to divorce. We don't know how often it occurred or what the legal causes for it were.

The practice of prostitution was extremely common in the Near East. In many cases it had a religious aspect. Houses of prostitution existed near the pagan temples. To have intercourse with a temple prostitute was to have communion with the goddess of the temple. The Book of Deuteronomy legislated against this practice in Israel (Dt 23:18), but not always successfully (1 K 14:24; 22:47; 2 K 23:7). The prophets regarded prostitution, religious or secular, as a sin (Am 2:7; Ho 4:14; Jr 5:7).

In the New Testament human sexuality is treated frankly and reverently. Jesus speaks of the pains of a woman in labor and of her joy once her child has been born (Jn 16:21). Elizabeth speaks of Jesus as the fruit of Mary's womb (Lk 1:42), and a woman blessed the womb that carried Jesus and the breasts that nursed him (Lk 11:27). Paul speaks of his labor pains until Christ was formed in the Galatians (Gal 4:19).

In the New Testament Jesus stated the need for purity of mind and heart and thought over and above purity of action: "Nothing that enters one from outside can defile that person; but the things that come out from within are what defile" (Mk 7:15). And he went on to say: "From within people, from their hearts, come evil thoughts, unchastity, theft, murder, adultery, greed, malice, deceit, licentiousness, envy, blasphemy, arrogance, folly. All these evils come from within and they defile" (Mk 7:20-23). In the same vein, Jesus said in his Sermon on the Mount: "You have heard it said, 'You shall not commit adultery.' But I say to you, everyone who looks at a woman with lust has already committed adultery with her in his heart" (Mt 5:27-28). God sees the heart, and judges men and women in accordance with what he finds in their hearts.

Jesus rejected the practice of divorce and remarriage, and reaffirmed the indissolubility of marriage as it was proclaimed in the Book of Genesis. He did so when he said to the Pharisees: "Have you not read that from the beginning the Creator 'made them male and female,' and said, 'For this reason a man shall leave his father and mother and be joined to his wife, and the two shall become one flesh'? So they are no longer two, but one flesh. Therefore what God has joined together, no human being must separate" (Mt 19:4-6). Jesus also approved the practice of celibacy "for the sake of the kingdom of heaven" (Mt 19:12). Jesus himself did not marry, although Jewish rabbis were expected to marry. The probable practice of celibacy among the Essenes, a Jewish sect, possibly forstalled any surprise or scandal at this state of affairs. Jesus promised that those who give up family and property to advance his cause would receive a hundred times more and inherit eternal life (Mt 19:29).

Paul followed his Master in rejecting divorce and remarriage (1 Cor 7:10-11). Paul held marriage to be a good thing because it had been created by God (1 Tm 4:1-5). He advised marriage so that men and women might not succumb to immorality in their weakness. Moreover, he did not recognize a double standard for husbands and wives. Just as a wife's body belongs to her husband, so a husband's body belongs to his wife. Each has an exclusive right in this matter (1 Cor 7:1-4). For Paul, married love should reflect the love of Christ for his Church. He wrote: "Husbands, love your wives even as Christ loved the church and handed himself over for her. . . . So [also] husbands should love their wives as their own bodies. He who loves his wife loves himself. For no one hates his own flesh but rather nourishes and cherishes it, even as Christ does the church" (Ep 5:25-29).

Paul also regarded the state of virginity and celibacy highly. Indeed that state was superior to marriage because it is an undivided attachment to the Lord, whereas married people must be anxious to please each other (1 Cor 7:32-35). Speaking to the unmarried and to widows, Paul said, "It is a good thing for them to remain as they are, as I do, but if they cannot exercise self-control they should marry" (1 Cor 7:8-9).

Paul's thoughts about human sexuality are also expressed by his forthright condemnation of unchastity, which he referred to several times as a vice. For example, he wrote: "Do not be deceived; neither fornicators nor idolaters nor adulterers nor boy prostitutes nor practicing homosexuals nor thieves nor the greedy nor drunkards nor slanderers nor robbers will inherit the kingdom of God" (1 Cor 6:9-10). Paul offered a profound reason for his condemnation of unchastity. "Avoid immorality," he wrote. "Every other sin a person commits is outside the body, but the immoral person sins against his own body. Do you not know that your body is a temple of the holy Spirit within you, whom you have from God, and that you are not your own? For you have been purchased at a price. Therefore glorify God in your body" (1 Cor 6:18-20).

QUESTIONS FOR REVIEW

1. According to the Old Testament what was the purpose of marriage and sexual activity?
2. What was the attitude of the Old Testament toward polygamy? Toward divorce? Toward prostitution?

3. Why did Jesus demand purity of mind and heart?
4. What did Jesus teach about divorce and remarriage?
5. What did Jesus think of celibacy?
6. What did Paul teach about marriage and chastity?

CHAPTER 47

Human Sexuality (II)
CHURCH TEACHING

On this occasion I wish to review the *Church's* teaching on human sexuality. The teaching of the Catholic Church is largely a restatement of Biblical teaching. The Church considers premarital intercourse a grave sin. For example, in 1245, the thirteenth ecumenical council of the Catholic Church held at Lyons in southern France had this to say: "There can be no doubt that fornication, which one unmarried person commits with another, is a mortal sin, since the Apostle Paul asserted that both fornicators and adulterers are excluded from the kingdom of God" (1 Cor 6:9).[1] Pope Pius XI reaffirmed this position in 1930 in a document beginning with the Latin words *Casti Connubii.* In this document, which dealt with Christian marriage, the Pope wrote: "Every use of the faculty given by God for the procreation of new life is the right and privilege of the married state alone, by the law of God and of nature, and must be confined absolutely within the sacred limits of that state."[2]

Catholic teaching about the purpose of marriage has undergone some development in recent years. In 1918, the

1 DS 835.
2 *Five Great Encyclicals* (New York: Paulist Press, 1939), 82.

official law book of the Catholic Church called the *Code of Canon Law* said this: "The primary purpose of marriage is the procreation and education of children. The secondary purpose of marriage is the mutual help [which husband and wife can give to each other] and the relief of concupiscence."[3] Then in 1951 Pope Pius XII stressed the personal values of marriage. Although these are not primary, the Pope said, they are nevertheless part of nature's plan and of great importance.[4]

In 1965 the Second Vatican Council also spoke about the purpose of marriage, but it avoided the language of primary and secondary purposes. According to the Council, the intimate partnership of married life and love has been established by the Creator and qualified by his laws. Marriage and married love are by nature ordained to the procreation and education of children. However, children are not the only purpose of marriage even if they are its crown. In virtue of their marriage, a husband and wife render companionship and service to each other through an intimate union of their persons and lives. The love of the spouses for each other leads them to a free and mutual gift of themselves. This love is uniquely expressed and perfected through the marital act. Jesus has raised the marriage between two baptized persons, who are of equal dignity, to the level of a sacrament, and it should never be profaned by adultery or divorce.[5]

In 1968, in a document beginning with the Latin words, *Humanae Vitae*, Pope Paul VI described in greater detail the love that should exist between a husband and his wife. That love is principally a matter of the will, although it involves the senses too; it is a total giving of oneself; it is faithful to one's partner and excludes all others until death; and it is open to the transmission of life. The marriage act itself has a twofold

3 Canon 1013.1
4 Pius XII, "Allocution to Midwives," Oct. 29, 1951, nos. 308-310.
5 Constitution on the Church in the Modern World, nos. 48-50.

significance, the unitive and procreative; that is to say, the act expresses and solidifies the union of husband and wife, and it looks to the generation of new life. The act should retain its twofold significance in all instances.[6]

The new *Code of Canon Law*, which was published in 1983 to reflect the teaching of the Second Vatican Council, puts the matter in this way: "The matrimonial covenant, by which a man and a woman undertake to share their lives together, is ordained by its very nature to the good of the spouses and the procreation and education of children. Christ the Lord has raised this covenant between baptized persons to the dignity of a sacrament."[7]

Since the Second Vatican Council described marriage as a partnership of life and love, Catholics have understood better the essential characteristics of a true marriage. If marriage is a partnership between husband and wife for life, then it involves their cohabitation in a way that is properly matrimonial. A husband and wife must have the mental, emotional, and psychological capacity to assume this partnership. It follows that "psychological impotence" along with physical impotence is an impediment to a real marriage.[8]

In 1976 the American Catholic bishops published a booklet dealing with the moral life of Catholics, titled *To Live in Christ Jesus.* In the booklet the bishops presented a summary of Church teaching on marriage and sexuality. The American bishops rejected the view that a marriage was dissolved simply because the love between a husband and wife had disappeared. They noted that a true marriage relationship exists not only on the biological level, but on all levels of personality. Then in four sentences the bishops succinctly stated the teaching of the Church on sexual morality:

6 *Humanea Vitae*, nos. 9, 12.
7 Canon 1055.1.
8 Cf. P.F. Palmer, "Marriage" in the *New Catholic Encyclopedia*, 16, 278-280.

"Our Christian tradition holds the sexual union between husband and wife in high honor. This union is a special expression of their love for each other, a love which mirrors God's love for his people and Christ's love for the Church. But like many things human, sex is ambivalent: it can be either creative or destructive. Sexual intercourse is a moral and human good only within marriage; outside marriage it is wrong."[9]

In the same booklet, they explained the Church's opposition to premarital and extramarital relations. Such relations are neither worthy of human beings nor are they in accordance with God's will. Such sinful relations lack the unconditional love of Christian marriage; they tend toward exploitation and self deception; they trivialize human sexuality; and they can erode the possibility of deep, lifelong commitments.

The virtue which regulates sexual activity in a reasonable way is chastity. Chastity is the virtue which disposes us to be pure in thought and deed. The demands of chastity are different for married and umarried persons. Married persons must exclude all others from their relationship, while unmarried persons must abstain from all sexual activity if they are to obey God's law. Sexual morality is the practice of Christian chastity. Chastity is a God-given adornment of human persons, a fruit of the action and presence of the Holy Spirit, as Paul writes (Gal 5:24).

In 1968 the American Catholic bishops wrote a pastoral letter called *Human Life in Our Day*. Speaking of chastity, they said: "The Christian asceticism of chastity, within and outside of marriage, honors the sanctity of life and protects the dignity of human sexuality. Were there no revelation nor religion, civilization itself would require rational discipline of the sexual instinct. Revelation, however, inspires chastity with more sublime purposes and creative power. In chaste

9 NCCB, *To Live in Christ Jesus* (Washington: USCC, 1968), 18-19.

love, the Christian, whether his vocation be to marriage or celibacy, expresses love for God himself."[10]

The cross of Christ has been planted at the very center of Christianity. The demands of chastity are indeed severe. The assaults upon chastity spring from many quarters. Some will despair of their ability to practice this virtue. Yet, as we know, God will not allow us to be tempted beyond our power to resist. His grace is sufficient for us. The grace of God lends clarity to the mind and strength to the will. We cooperate with the grace of God by avoiding the occasions of sin — those persons, places, and things that lead us into sin. We invite the grace of God by fidelity to our religious duties, especially the frequent reception of the sacraments of penance and the Eucharist. In this as in so many other matters, we are vividly conscious of our own weakness, yet humbly reliant on God's mercy.

10 NCCB, *Human Life in Our Day* (Washington: USCC, 1968), 9.

QUESTIONS FOR REVIEW

1. Why must the use of sexual faculties be confined to marriage?
2. What is the purpose of marriage?
3. What is the significance of the marriage act?
4. Why is "psychological impotence" an impediment to marriage?
5. Why does a marriage continue to exist even after love disappears?
6. Why are premarital and extramarital sexual relations wrong?
7. What is chastity?
8. How can a person be chaste in the modern world?

CHAPTER 48

Human Sexuality (III)
CHASTITY

The teaching of the Catholic Church about sexuality is largely a restatement of Biblical teaching. On the last occasion I said a word about chastity. Now I should like to say something more about it. Chastity is the virtue which regulates sexual activity in a reasonable way. The demands of chastity are different for married and unmarried persons. Sexual morality is the practice of Christian chastity. Chastity extends to thoughts, words, and deeds.

The challenge which faces all persons in practicing chastity stems from original sin and the strength of sexual desires. Moreover, we live in an atmosphere of sex. Sex is the interminable theme of so many novels, advertisements, popular songs, movies, and television programs. The atmosphere of sex can create a false impression — that the differences between men and women exist solely for the sake of pleasure, that one may exploit these differences outside of marriage. The atmosphere of sex is a kind of pollution that clouds our moral judgment and enervates the strength of our convictions.

The initial challenge to chastity comes from the imagination. The imagination can conjure up sexual fantasies in the married and unmarried alike. The imagination is unruly and it often acts without our consent. However, consent is crucial to the preservation of chastity. If one calmly seeks to dispel the impure fantasies of the imagination, then there is no guilt, no violation of chastity. But if one does nothing to dispel the impure fantasies of the imagination and entertains them willingly, then there is guilt, even grave guilt, and a violation of chastity. Here we have the lustful thoughts and desires which Our Savior condemned in his Sermon on the Mount (Mt 5:27-28).

Then there are the external actions of kissing, embracing, and touching. If these actions produce merely the warmth and satisfaction that relates to male-female companionship, then they are not sinful even where unmarried persons are concerned. On the other hand, these actions may be prolonged to the point of genital or venereal pleasure. In this case they become sinful where unmarried persons are concerned. It is the traditional teaching of the Church that unmarried persons may not actively seek or consent to genital or venereal pleasure. For them to do so is to sin gravely. This pleasure is reserved to married persons. In the case of married persons, actions like kissing, embracing, and touching with the concomitant pleasure are to be encouraged.

Finally, there is the complete act of sexual intercourse. According to Catholic teaching, it is a good and praiseworthy act within marriage. Adultery, however, is gravely sinful; a man must be faithful to his wife just as Christ is faithful to the Church. Premarital sex is gravely sinful; two unmarried people have no right to the marriage act. The Church also teaches that masturbation and homosexual actions are gravely sinful.

By this time the attentive reader will understand that no violation of chastity is trivial. In other words, every direct violation of chastity is gravely sinful when it is committed with sufficient reflection and full consent of the will. This statement applies not only to the complete act of sexual intercourse outside of marriage, but also to incomplete acts between unmarried people which include sexual gratification. By incomplete acts in this case I mean prolonged kissing, embracing, and touching. Such incomplete acts are gravely sinful because they place the unmarried couple without justification in danger of going all the way. There is a natural dynamism that links even the initial forms of sexual stimulation to the complete act of sexual intercourse in which they reach a climax.

In 1975 the Sacred Congregation for the Doctrine of the Faith, an agency of the Pope, wrote a document called *A Declaration on Sexual Ethics.* In that document the Congregation reaffirmed the teaching of the Church that "the moral order of sexuality involves such high values of human life that every direct violation of this order is objectively serious." The Congregation went on to say, however: "In sins of the sexual order, in view of their kind and their causes, it more easily happens that free consent is not fully given; this is a fact which calls for caution when judging a person's responsibility. In this matter it is particularly opportune to recall the following words of Scripture: 'Man looks at appearances, but God looks at the heart' " (1 S 16:7).[1]

In this matter of chastity a particular difficulty confronts two young people who are planning to marry. How can such a couple grow and develop in their relationship without engaging in forbidden sexual activity? Some would say that such a couple has a right to sexual union even before marriage, provided they intend to marry, but cannot marry in the near future. Some would see sexual intercourse in this context as a means of building and preserving their relationship. However, this opinion is contrary to Christian doctrine which states that every genital act must be within the framework of marriage. Even though the couple's intention to marry may be firm, it is still subject to revocation. The relationship between the couple is not yet totally exclusive, permanent, and possessive; therefore, genital activity itself is not warranted.

I remarked earlier that unmarried people may not actively

1 No. 10.

seek or consent to venereal pleasure. This principle applies to engaged couples too. However, an engaged couple needs to foster their relationship. Two young people who have practiced chastity as single persons will have to overcome certain defenses and inhibitions built up over the years with respect to the opposite sex. They have good reason for deeply affectionate kisses, touches, and embraces. *Unintended* venereal pleasure can result, but being unintended, it is not sinful. Two young persons planning to marry should bear two things in mind — they need to express their love for each other in a physical way, yet they must be aware of the powerful force of the sexual drive which can carry them away if they are not prudent. Only mature persons can handle this situation successfully, but that's the kind of persons I am talking to.

In order to lead a chaste life young people must use the means which have always been recommended by the Church. These means are discipline of the senses and mind: watchfulness and prudence in avoiding the occasions of sin, the observance of modesty, moderation in recreation, wholesome pursuits, assiduous prayer, and frequent reception of the sacraments of penance and the Holy Eucharist. Young people should keep before their eyes the chaste lives of Jesus, his mother Mary, and the saints who excelled in the practice of chastity.

Spiritual writers and preachers have frequently observed that while Jesus allowed himself to be accused of many crimes, such as breaking the Law of Moses, or stirring up civil strife, or uttering blasphemy, he never allowed himself to be accused of unchastity. For his disciples he chose men, married and unmarried, who before their conversion were shortsighted, vain, cowardly, and weak in many respects. Yet, we never read in the Scriptures that they were guilty of any failings in this matter of chastity.

In conclusion, I should like to refer once more to *A Declaration on Sexual Ethics*. There we find a summary of our common responsibility to create a climate in which chastity is appreciated and fostered. As teachers of the faith, bishops must proclaim the traditional principles of sexual morality. These principles are by no means out-of-date. Actually they are in complete harmony with the divine order of creation, the spirit of Christ, and the dignity of human nature. The bishops and their priest-collaborators will have to proclaim these principles in the face of much disbelief and contradiction.

Parents and teachers must endeavor to lead their children and pupils to the psychological, emotional, and moral maturity befitting their age. Parents and teachers will instruct young people in accordance with their age, and they will reinforce this instruction by the example of their own lives. Parents and teachers will have to protect the young from many dangers of which they are unaware.

Artists, writers, and those who employ the modern means of communication have a great responsibility in view of the enormous influence they can have. They may not sacrifice the principles of morality for the sake of artistic purposes or material gain. Whether it be a case of artistic or literary works, public entertainment, or providing information, each individual must show tact, discretion, moderation, and a true sense of values. In this way, each one can contribute to the health of the moral climate. For their part, all lay men and women should endeavor to act in the same way.[2]

2 No. 13.

QUESTIONS FOR REVIEW

1. What is chastity?
2. Whence arises the challenge to chastity?

3. When do the impure fantasies of the imagination become sinful?
4. When do kissing, embracing, and touching become sinful?
5. Why is no direct violation of chastity trivial?
6. How should an engaged couple conduct themselves with respect each other?
7. How does one preserve chastity?
8. What can we all do to create a climate in which chastity is appreciated and fostered?

CHAPTER 49

Human Sexuality (IV)
HOMOSEXUALITY AND MASTURBATION

Today I wish to take up two problems connected with sexuality, the problem of homosexuality and the problem of self-gratification known as masturbation. First, the problem of homosexuality.

What is homosexuality? Homosexuality is a condition or disposition whereby a person is attracted erotically to persons of the same sex and is repelled by physical relations with the opposite sex. There is a temporary homosexuality which is usually due to a specific environment, such as that found in prisons, army camps, and boarding schools; but here we are talking about a persistent and enduring orientation. Homosexuality exists in varying degrees in both males and females. Persons having this disposition may or may not engage in homosexual activity. The homosexual's aversion from physical relationships with the opposite sex does not preclude warm friendship. It is difficult to estimate the incidence of homosexuality in the general population but it seems to be quite small.

What causes homosexuality? We just don't know. It seems clear, however, that the basic cause of homosexuality is psychological, that the condition arises early in life without a conscious decision on the part of the person so oriented. Such an orientation, therefore, need have no moral significance; it is simply something that happened beyond that person's control. As one Catholic teacher put it, "Homosexual orientation entails no more sin than shortness or tallness. Is such an orientation a good thing in itself? No, objectively speaking, it is a deficiency, a disorder, but not a sin."[1]

Whereas homosexual *orientation* is not a sin, homosexual *activity* is. The American Catholic bishops made this point in a pastoral letter written in 1976. The bishops wrote: "Homosexual activity, as distinguished from homosexual orientation, is morally wrong. Like heterosexual persons, homosexual persons are called to give witness to chastity. They must avoid with God's grace behavior which is wrong for them, just as nonmarital sexual relations are wrong for heterosexuals."[2]

The teaching of the American Catholic bishops about the immorality of homosexual activity reflects the constant tradition of the Church. That tradition links genital sexual activity with the transmission of life within a monogamous marriage between a man and a woman. The homosexual act is incapable of transmitting life to another person; therefore, it is an inordinate use of the sexual faculty and morally wrong.

The teaching of the American Catholic bishops about homosexuality reflects the teaching of the Bible. Nowhere in the Bible do we read that the homosexual person is condemned, but always the action is condemned. For example, we read in the Book of Leviticus: "You shall not lie with a male as with a woman; such a thing is an abomination" (Lv 18:22). And in the New Testament we understand from Paul that "neither fornicators nor idolaters nor adulterers nor boy prostitutes nor practicing homosexuals . . . will inherit the kingdom of God" (1

1 Archbishop Daniel E. Pilarczyk, writing in the Catholic Telegram, Cincinnati, Ohio, April 1, 1988, p. 7.

2 NCCB, To Live in Christ Jesus (Washington: USCC, 1976), 19.

Cor 6:9-10). The Bible supposes that a proper sexual union joins a male and female.

Even though homosexual activity is objectively a grave sin, it is not gravely sinful when it lacks truly free consent. Erotic fantasies and desires can arise without consent and induce apparently compulsive behavior. Like all of us, however, homosexual persons must do what they can to live chaste lives. They must avoid the occasions of sin, those persons, places, and things that lead them into sin. They should seek the counsel of an experienced confessor or psychiatrist. They should try to form friendships with both homosexuals and heterosexuals. They should break out of homosexual environments and reintegrate themselves into heterosexual culture. Like all of us, homosexual persons may rely on the grace of the Holy Spirit to live a chaste life. Chastity is a gift from God which he does not deny to those who ask properly. Paul wrote to the Corinthians that God "is faithful and will not let you be tried beyond your strength; but with the trial he will also provide a way out, so that you may be able to bear it" (1 Cor 10:13).

Society must bear in mind that homosexual persons enjoy the same human dignity that others enjoy. The Son of God died on Calvary for them as he did for other human beings. Homosexual orientation does not deprive one of God's love, and God offers his forgiveness to one who repents of homosexual behavior. Society errs grievously when it supposes that all homosexual persons are oversexed, that they constitute a threat to the innocent, that they are incapable of honorable friendship with others. Violence and abuse directed against known or suspected homosexual persons are wrong. It is wrong to deprive a person of employment exclusively on the ground of that person's sexual orientation.

At the beginning of my talk on this occasion I said that I wished to deal with two problems, the problem of homosexuality and the problem of masturbation. Now I wish to say a word about the latter problem. Masturbation is also called self-abuse, self-pollution, and onanism, and it means self-stimulation to sexual climax. It is not clear that the Bible passes judgment on this act, but the traditional teaching of the Church holds that masturbation is seriously wrong in an objective sense, even in individual instances. The reason is that it is a use of the sexual faculty outside of marriage. Earlier I recalled the teaching of the Church that God intended the sexual faculty to be used within marriage for the procreation of children. Within marriage self-stimulation of the sexual faculty is lawful only in connection with the natural act of intercourse.

Objectively, therefore, masturbation is a grave moral disorder, but we may not conclude that it always involves grave sin on the subjective level. To be guilty of grave sin one must freely perform some act which he or she knows to be seriously evil. As a matter of fact, impulse, habits, and circumstance can impair one's judgment and freedom, so that one masturbates without serious guilt. Compulsive masturbation could be a sign of other emotional and mental disorders. In general, however, we may not presume a lack of responsibility for masturbatory acts. Such a presumption does not do justice to one's moral capacity.

The frequency of masturbation, especially among adolescents, derives from many sources including the innate weakness of human nature as the result of original sin, the loss of the sense of God, the corruption of morals engendered by the commercialization of vice, the blatant licentiousness of so many public entertainments and publications, as well as the neglect of modesty which is the guardian of chastity.[3]

How is a person to judge the gravity of masturbation in concrete instances? To answer this question, one must take

3 Cf. Congregation for the Doctrine of the Faith, *A Declaration on Sexual Ethics* (Washington: USCC, 1976), no. 9.

into account the habitual behavior of those who are troubled by this disorder. Do they try to lead an upright life in general? Do they observe the other precepts of chastity? Do they use the means, both natural and supernatural, which are recommended by Christian asceticism for governing the passions and progressing in virtue? An affirmative answer to these questions will suggest that an act of masturbation was involuntary or semivoluntary and without serious guilt. Furthermore, what takes place spontaneously during sleep cannot involve guilt. What takes place just before going to sleep or immediately upon waking in a sleepy state hardly involves full deliberation.

How is a young person who is troubled by this problem going to deal with it? There are several things he can do:

First, he can seek advice about his problem. Not to seek advice because of shame or attachment to the sin leaves one mired in the mud. A counselor or a confessor can offer advice. Such advice should aim at discovering and responding to the cause of such behavior. If one eliminates the cause, then one eliminates the effect.

Second, the young person who is tempted to masturbate should seek to become less self-centered and engage in activities that are centered on others. I think an interest in sports can help in this regard.

Third, there are spiritual remedies. I am thinking of the determination to love God and avoid what offends him, prayer, and the reception of the sacraments.

Fourth, one must avoid the occasions of sin, those persons, places, and things that lead us into it. Pornographic movies and publications are occasions of sin; thus, they should be avoided.

Finally, the young person who is troubled by this disorder should remember that God never permits us to be tempted beyond our strength to resist. At the outset, resistance may prove unsuccessful; but in this matter as in so many others, perseverance pays off. Along with the test God will show the way out (1 Cor 10:13)

QUESTIONS FOR REVIEW

1. What is homosexuality?
2. What is the origin of homosexual orientation?
3. Why is homosexual activity wrong?
4. What helps are available to the homosexual to lead a moral life?
5. What is masturbation?
6. Why is masturbation a serious disorder?
7. How can one judge the subjective guilt of a person who masturbates?
8. How can one troubled by masturbation overcome it?

CHAPTER 50

Human Sexuality (V)
BIRTH CONTROL AND ARTIFICIAL CONCEPTION

I wish to conclude my talks on human sexuality by discussing two subjects, namely, birth control and artificial conception or artificial techniques of procreation. First, I wish to take up the subject of birth control.

By birth control I mean regulation of the number of children born, especially by preventing or lessening the frequency of conception. The problem of birth control did not originate in the twentieth century. Earlier centuries and civilizations were also concerned with it. However, the population explosion, the development of modern contraceptives, and the shift from an agrarian economy where large families were an economic asset to an industrial and technological economy have all magnified the birth control problem.

Catholic teaching does not demand that Catholic couples have as many children as they can. It is up to the parents themselves to decide how large their family is going to be. They will make this decision by taking into account their own welfare, that of the children, and the interests of society and the Church. However, it does make a difference *how* a married couple regulates the size of their family. In this matter, a couple cannot proceed arbitrarily. They must be governed by the law of God which is interpreted by the teaching authority of the Church in the light of the gospel.[1]

There are of course illegitimate means of regulating the size of one's family. Abortion is one of them; sterilization, whether of the husband or the wife, is another; and artificial contraception is a third. The latter, artificial contraception, was the partial subject of an encyclical letter, *Humanae Vitae*, written by Pope Paul VI in 1968. Following an age-old teaching of the Catholic Church, Pope Paul VI taught that artificial contraception was an illegitimate means of birth control. In his letter, the Pope analyzed the nature and meaning of the conjugal act as it was designed by the Creator. The conjugal act closely unites husband and wife and makes them capable of generating new life. To interfere with the life-giving potentiality of the conjugal act is to contradict its meaning and purpose and oppose the plan and will of God. Each and every conjugal act, therefore, must be open to the transmission of life. It follows, the Pope concluded, that every action, such as artificial contraception, which renders the transmission of life impossible, is immoral.[2]

Some married couples justify the use of artificial contraception on the grounds that it fosters a more loving relationship. It does so, they say, because it eliminates the fear of an unwanted pregnancy. Still, it does not seem that contraception leads to more stable marriages. Indeed, in a society where contraception is widespread, the opposite appears to be the case.

In itself, therefore, artificial contraception is an illegitimate means of birth control. Yet, as I have suggested, many couples truly believe that it is a legitimate means of birth control. It is not easy to understand the immorality of the practice under the pressures of married life. Are those couples

1 Cf. Vatican II, Constitution on the Church in the Modern World, no. 50.
2 Cf. *Humanae Vitae*, no. 13.

who innocently practice artificial contraception more fortunate than those who know about the teaching of the Church? I don't think so. Actions that violate the law of God, whether the violation is conscious or unconscious, take their toll in the long run.

There is, however, a legitimate means of regulating the size of one's family. It is called natural family planning. We all know that there are times when a married woman cannot conceive a child. If, for legitimate reasons, a couple chooses to have intercourse only at these times, they act lawfully. They are making legitimate use of a natural disposition, whereas contraception impedes the development of a natural process.[3]

Does natural family planning work? Yes, it does. Just as methods of artificial contraception have been improved, so methods of natural family planning have been improved. They can be as effective as any chemical contraceptive. Moreover, a couple can learn the technique of natural family planning without excessive difficulty. Any pastoral minister connected with a local parish can tell a couple where this technique can be learned. It is true that natural family planning requires a certain degree of self-discipline, that is to say, periods of abstinence from intercourse for a week or two each month. However, the rewards of natural family planning are considerable — not the least being a whole new dimension of communication and bonding between the married couple.

Earlier I said that I wish to discuss not only birth control, but also artificial conception or artificial techniques of procreation. By the latter I mean achieving human conception in a manner other than the sexual union of a man and woman. Human conception can come about through artificial insemination, that is to say, by artificially injecting sperm from a man into the genital tracts of a woman. Moreover, what was once regarded as science fiction is now a fact. Scientists can now

3 Cf. *Humanae Vitae*, no. 16.

produce a new human being in a laboratory. A scientist can fertilize a human egg with a human sperm in a laboratory dish, and then implant the fertilized egg in a woman. The egg may come from the wife of a married couple or from another woman; the sperm may come from the wife's husband or from another man. The fertilized egg can be implanted in the wife or in another woman who acts as a surrogate mother in whom the embryo develops.

Needless to say, we are not talking here about a medical procedure which facilitates the conception of a child by enabling the normal act of marital intercourse to achieve its purpose. Such a medical procedure is perfectly legitimate. No, we are talking here about the conception of a child without the sexual union of husband and wife.

What is the attitude of the Church toward artificial human procreation? The Church rejects it as something contrary to the nature of human beings and marriage. Following the teaching of the Bible and its own lengthy tradition, the Church holds that children must be the fruit of marriage, that they must be conceived by the conjugal acts of husband and wife in accordance with the laws inscribed in their persons and in their union. Therefore, the generation of new life without the simultaneous and direct cooperation of husband and wife is contrary to the nature of human beings and marriage.[4] From these principles one must conclude that artificial insemination and fertilization in a laboratory (often called *in vitro* fertilization) are wrong whether they are done inside or outside of marriage. Indeed, fertilization by a man other than the wife's husband seems to take on the deformity of adultery, even if she and her husband consent to the procedure.

Surely the Church's teaching about the immorality of artificial methods of procreation is a difficult one for couples

4 Cf. Instruction on *Respect for Human Life in Its Origin* by the Congregation for the Doctrine of the Faith, 1987.

who cannot have children. It is natural for a couple to desire a child. Marriage, however, does not confer upon the couple the right to have a child, but only the right to perform those natural acts which normally lead to procreation. We must remember that a child is not an object to be owned. A child is a gift, the supreme gift, of God. "For this reason, the child has the right to be the fruit of the specific act of conjugal love of his parents; and he also has the right to be respected as a person from the moment of his conception."[5] We must also note that even without the possibility of children, married life does not lose its value; and childless couples can do much for others, including the adoption of children and assistance to poor and handicapped children.

My discussion of artificial techniques of procreation recalls a principle of Catholic practice which has many applications. The principle states that we may not act wrongly in order to achieve a good purpose. A couple's desire for a child is proper and good, but they may not use any means whatsoever to fulfill that desire. Just because we can do something does not make that something morally right.

Surely civil authorities have a responsibility in this matter. They have a responsibility to promote the common good and proscribe what is harmful to the welfare of citizens. Consequently, they should legislate against the artificial insemination of women and the creation of human beings in a laboratory. Unquestionably not all citizens in modern democracies share this view, but those citizens who are better informed will work to educate and reform public opinion.

I close my remarks on this occasion with a question asked by Pope John Paul II in his first encyclical letter, *Redemptor Hominis*. There he wrote: "We must ask ourselves, with absolute honesty, objectivity, and a sense of moral responsibility, the essential questions concerning man's situation today and

5 *Ibid.*, no. 8.

in the future. Do all the conquests attained until now and those projected for the future for technology accord with man's moral and spiritual progress? In this context is man, as man, developing and progressing or is he regressing and being degraded in his humanity?"[6]

6 *Redemptor Hominis* (1979), no. 48.

QUESTIONS FOR REVIEW

1. How should parents determine the size of their family?
2. Why is artificial contraception wrong?
3. Why is natural family planning a legitimate means of regulating the size of one's family?
4. What are artificial techniques of procreation?
5. Why are they wrong?
6. May we do evil that good may come of it?

An Interesting Thought

The publication you have just finished reading is part of the apostolic efforts of the Society of St. Paul of the American Province. The Society of St. Paul is an international religious community located in 23 countries, whose particular call and ministry is to bring the message of Christ to all people through the communications media.

Following in the footsteps of their patron, St. Paul the Apostle, priests and brothers blend a life of prayer and technology as writers, editors, marketing directors, graphic designers, bookstore managers, pressmen, sound engineers, etc. in the various fields of the mass media, to announce the message of Jesus.

If you know a young man who might be interested in a religious vocation as a brother or priest and who shows talent and skill in the communications arts, ask him to consider our life and ministry. For more information at no cost or obligation write:

Vocation Office
2187 Victory Blvd.
Staten Island, NY 10314-6603
Telephone: (718) 698-3698